Our History Is Still Being Written

Our History Is Still Being Written

THE STORY OF THREE CHINESE CUBAN GENERALS IN THE CUBAN REVOLUTION

ARMANDO CHOY ● GUSTAVO CHUI ● MOISÉS SÍO WONG

Pathfinder

NEW YORK   LONDON   MONTREAL   SYDNEY

Edited by Mary-Alice Waters

Copyright © 2005, 2017 by Pathfinder Press
All rights reserved

ISBN 978-1-60488-102-8
Library of Congress Control Number 2017960740
Manufactured in United States of America

First edition, 2005
Second edition, 2017

COVER DESIGN: Eva Braiman
COVER PHOTO: Members of Chinese New Democracy Alliance at
    Havana rally, September 2, 1960. Organized in response to
    Washington's efforts to line up Latin American governments
    against Cuba, the rally of more than one million approved
    a reply to the US rulers known as the First Declaration of
    Havana. Banner says: "Resident Chinese support the Cuban
    Revolution and its leader, Fidel Castro!"

Pathfinder
www.pathfinderpress.com
E-mail: pathfinder@pathfinderpress.com

Contents

Maps

Boxes, Photos, Illustrations

Preface to second edition

MARY-ALICE WATERS

THIS NEW EDITION OF *Our History Is Still Being Written: The Story of Three Chinese Cuban Generals in the Cuban Revolution* appears twelve years after the original was presented at the Havana International Book Fair in February 2006. The demand for a second edition is testimony to the enduring interest engendered by the rich history of revolutionary struggle—and victories—brought to life through the words of Armando Choy, Gustavo Chui, and Moisés Sío Wong.

In the years since Pathfinder Press first published their accounts, in Spanish and an English translation, the book has been the centerpiece of more than a hundred presentations and panel discussions in countries, cities, and universities around the globe—from Santiago de Cuba to Beijing and Guangzhou; from Kuala Lumpur to Caracas; from Vancouver, Toronto, and Montreal to San Francisco, New York, Miami, London, Edinburgh, Auckland, and Sydney, to name just a few.

A Chinese translation was published in 2008 by the Intellec-

Mary-Alice Waters, president of Pathfinder Press, is the editor of *New International*, a magazine of Marxist politics and theory. She has edited more than thirty books of interviews, writings, and speeches of leaders of the Cuban Revolution.

tual Property Publishing House; a Cuban edition by Editora Política in 2010; and one in Farsi by the Iranian publisher Talaye Porsoo in 2014. A French translation of this new edition is set for 2018.

Three facts above all, unexpected to most readers, have generated this broad interest.

First, many learn with surprise that Cuba was a major destination of the large-scale Chinese emigration in the nineteenth century known historically as the "coolie trade." Readers are stunned to discover that more than 140,000 bonded laborers were shipped from South China seaports to Cuba between 1847 and 1874—imported at the demand of wealthy plantation owners to replace dwindling African slave labor in the cane fields of what was then the largest sugar-producing country in the world.

As a percentage of the population, this Chinese immigration was greater than anywhere else in the Americas. In those same years, it was proportionally larger than the influx into the United States of Chinese toilers, who first came to California in search of gold and then to build the most daunting segment of the history-altering transcontinental railroad.

With few exceptions, the indentured workers who survived the sea voyage to Cuba, and then eight years of contracted labor under conditions akin to slavery, never returned to China. They intermarried, became laborers, small farmers, and petty traders. They lived as other Cuban working people did. Today on the streets of Havana and other cities across the island, it is not unusual to be told that the Cuban nation was born with the intertwining of three strands—one Spanish, one African, and one Chinese.

Second, readers are surprised by the massive participation and exemplary contribution of Chinese workers in Cuba's wars for independence from Spain between 1868 and 1898, wars inextricably interlinked with the struggle to abolish slavery and bonded labor in all forms. As Sío Wong's account underscores, nothing like it occurred in any other part of the world where large numbers of Chinese workers settled.

Third, and most important, many readers are stunned to learn that in Cuba today, unlike anywhere else on earth, discrimination and even prejudice against Cubans of Chinese descent have virtually ceased to exist. There is no glass ceiling, no sector of society or level of responsibility where only token Chinese Cubans can be found. There are no typically "Chinese jobs." Wang Lusha speaks eloquently to this question in the foreword to this new edition that follows.

How is this possible? Why is the Chinese community in Cuba different from Peru, Brazil, Argentina, or North America, Sío Wong asks. "The difference," he answers, "is the triumph of a socialist revolution." Here "we overturned the property relations that create not only economic but also social inequality between rich and poor. That is what made it possible for the son of Chinese immigrants to become a government representative, or anything else."

Our History Is Still Being Written is in fact an introduction to that socialist revolution.

How and why young Cubans like the three authors joined the revolutionary struggle to overthrow what working people there simply called "the tyranny" in the 1950s: the US-backed police dictatorship of Fulgencio Batista.

How and why the triumph of that immense popular struggle—one that cost 20,000 lives—opened the road to the first socialist revolution in the Americas.

How in making that revolution, millions of men and women, young and old, transformed themselves as they fought to lay the foundations of a new economic and social order.

Why the Cuban Revolution remains today the only living example of what a socialist revolution is and what ordinary working people, like those who made it and continue to defend it, can accomplish.

The most important single addition to the second edition of *Our History Is Still Being Written* is the foreword by Chinese translator Wang Lusha, originally published as an afterword to the 2008 Chinese edition. He explains how he first learned about the three Chinese Cuban generals, and the impact their stories had on his life. Wang gives voice to the surprise and pride of many Chinese around the world, especially young people, who through this book have come to know more of their own history of revolutionary resistance, combat, and victory.

Our thanks go to Linette Chua in Manila for translating the foreword to English, and to José Ignacio Fernández Armas and Kagita Chen Xiulian in Havana for its translation to Spanish.

In this new edition of the book, some translations have been improved. Footnotes have been added to clarify references rendered obscure by the passage of more than a decade, and biographical details in the authors' notes and glossary have been updated. New photos and illustrations have been added, as well.

Most important, the powerful revolutionary message of Armando Choy, Gustavo Chui, and Moisés Sío Wong, in their own words, remains unchanged.

December 2017

Jonathan Silberman/Militant

"This book will help get out the truth about the Cuban Revolution in every country," said General Moisés Sío Wong, speaking at Havana launching of *Our History Is Still Being Written*, February 2006. "And it will help people learn about the role of Chinese in Cuban history."

Other speakers at the Havana event included, from left: Cuban vice president José Ramón Fernández, General Gustavo Chui, and General Armando Choy.

The book has been presented at more than 100 meetings in cities around the world.

Foreword

WANG LUSHA

FOR CHINESE BORN AFTER the 1970s, Cuba remains a foreign and unfamiliar country. We know very little about its geographical location, its customs and traditions, its history and culture. Maybe our only impression of Cuba comes from that iconic image of Che Guevara, sporting a black beret with a five-pointed star, emblazoned on T-shirts. So, what *is* the real significance of Cuba for us?

When I was growing up, I often heard my father talk about how, during the prime of his youth, he took part in protests against the Americans. During street rallies they would chant *"Cuba sí, yanquis no!"* in support of the Cuban Revolution and against the US blockade. The song "Beautiful Havana" was a huge hit in China back then. Many young people were captivated by the charisma of Che Guevara, Fidel Castro, and other Cuban leaders. Cuba, with its unique attraction, touched and inspired an entire generation of Chinese youth.

Yet, with the passage of time, new generations in China have seemingly forgotten Cuba—this faraway country sit-

Wang Lusha translated the Chinese edition of this book, published in Beijing in 2008. He works in the Chinese film and TV industry, and was the scriptwriter for a 28-part TV series on the Chinese in Cuba. He lives in Huhehaote, Inner Mongolia, and in Beijing.

uated in the Caribbean—a land that had once immensely
stirred our great national pride and spirit. But the history of
Cuba is still being written by generation after generation of
Cubans. This history, while unknown to young Chinese, has
not been forgotten by the rest of the world. People around the
globe seeking freedom and justice continue to look to this
promised land called Cuba. And one of them is the American
journalist Mary-Alice Waters. She conceived this book with a
deep passion for Cuba. I hope my translation is able to convey
this feeling to all Chinese who are similarly interested and
want to know more about Cuba.

■

Although I have not traveled or walked every inch of this
earth, nor do I claim to be highly experienced and knowl-
edgeable, I lived for five years in the Netherlands in the northern region of the globe and in New Zealand at the opposing
southern end. Those years allowed me to learn a little about
Western civilization and gain a deeper understanding of the
lives of the Chinese overseas.

Two things stand out vividly in my memory. The first
was in New Zealand when I visited a cultural exhibit on
Chinese immigration, which featured many derogatory
cartoons drawn by Westerners a century ago. The Chinese
were mainly depicted with buck teeth, sporting a pigtail,
two small tufts of mustache, slit eyes, and long fingernails.
People who saw these drawings would easily view Chinese
as nasty and treacherous villains. Most of the drawings
portrayed Chinese as foreigners coming to New Zealand
to open laundries or restaurants, or to work as coolies, thus
forcing many New Zealanders out of work or out of business.

Today, while the status of the Chinese in the West has improved considerably, the stereotype still exists that Chinese are only good at two things: running a restaurant and doing math. (The reason Chinese are superior to others in math is because of the strong basic education established by the Chinese government in the aftermath of the "Cultural Revolution." Beginning in primary school, students are not allowed to use calculators—they are taught to do math with pencil and paper.)

The second thing that remains fresh in my memory is my conversation with an African classmate from Cameroon while I was studying in the Netherlands. After learning that I came from China, he told me there were a lot of Chinese in his country, adding that I must be a good cook. I found it very strange and asked him what made him think that. He replied that all the Chinese in his country open restaurants, so he concluded that we must all be excellent cooks. Fortunately he didn't think cooking was the *only* thing we can do. It seems that, from the most advanced countries such as the United States to the underdeveloped continent of Africa, all Chinese are seen as engaging in the culinary profession.

During my few years living abroad, I too worked in a restaurant, and almost every compatriot I have met abroad has done the same (including those born and raised in the Netherlands and New Zealand). So is cooking the only thing we are capable of? No. There's now another career Chinese are also considered good at—computer programming. That's because it requires basic math skills.

The reality is that many overseas Chinese are exceedingly wealthy, yet they are still not given recognition or accepted by the society, much less by the government of the countries where they live. For a time I was sad that I had been born Chinese. I wished I'd had an American father because I became fixated on one thing—that Americans are highly regarded and sought after all over the world, while in contrast, Chinese are seen as incompetent and inferior.

But one man changed my way of thinking and made me reconsider everything. That man was General Moisés Sío Wong. The first article I read about him online introduced him as a Chinese descendant in Cuba who through his own efforts became a general and even served as adjutant to Raúl Castro. That couldn't be true, I thought. A Chinese Cuban general? Humph! How is that possible? Chinese in other countries are only suitable for working in a kitchen—how can they go past the chopping block and become leaders? I used to have this view. However, my long-suppressed national pride and dignity pushed me to quietly search on my own for more information about General Sío Wong.

Fortunately, by pure coincidence I discovered this book, *Our History Is Still Being Written*. Through interviews with General Sío Wong as well as Armando Choy and Gustavo Chui, the two other Chinese Cuban generals, the book presents the modern history of Cuba from a unique perspective.

I felt overwhelmed as I read through the pages of the book. I discovered that, in addition to General Sío Wong, there are many other Chinese who made remarkable contributions in Cuba. They played important roles not only in the economic field but in the political arena. These included José Wong, José Bu, José Tolón (Lai Wa), Armando Choy, Gustavo Chui, and many more. Together, these Chinese Cubans added a powerful and compelling chapter to the history of Chinese overseas.

It seems then that Chinese were not born to be cooks! Nor are we inferior to other nationalities. There is nothing sad or shameful about being born Chinese! So I asked myself, what happened in Cuba that gave Chinese the status and positions they enjoy today, something they are denied in other countries?

General Sío Wong in this book explains: "[In Cuba] a socialist revolution took place. The revolution uprooted discrimination based on the color of a person's skin. That's because, above all, we overturned the property relations that create not only economic but also social inequality between rich and poor."

This is what the socialist revolution has given us—the elimination of the foundations of racism and class inequality. This is also why all foreigners in China today are treated fairly and hospitably, regardless of their skin color or wealth. This is the greatness of the socialist revolution!

Through interviews with General Sío Wong, General Choy, and General Chui, the book, *Our History Is Still Being Written*, narrates their experiences during the socialist revolution in Cuba and describes the country before and after the revolution. As they speak to us in their own words of the struggles and hardships of Chinese Cubans, they also provide us with a telling insight—the Chinese never saw themselves as a race separate from the Cuban people, but rather as fighting together with Fidel Castro, Che Guevara, and other Cubans in the struggle for the liberation of their country. In a socialist revolution there are no racial differences, only hands that strive and fight for freedom.

■

I would like to thank my parents for their continuous support and help in my life and studies abroad. I would also like to express my gratitude to television director Wang Xinmin for his guidance and encouragement, as well as to producers Zhang Mingzhi and Liu Xiangqun for their trust and for providing me with the English edition of *Our History is Still Being Written*. I thank Mr. Liu Guohua for all the information

on the history of Cuba, Cao Na and Li Wenming for their
invaluable assistance during the translation process, Wang
Ludi and Meng Ran for translating Spanish portions of the
book, and Ms. Wang Ping for proofreading my work. I want
to convey my appreciation to everyone who understood and
supported me throughout the entire project. Without all of
you, I would never have succeeded in translating this book.
Thank you!

2008

Introduction

MARY-ALICE WATERS

Our History Is Still Being Written adds one more chapter to the chronicle of the Cuban Revolution as told by those who have been on the front lines of that epic battle for more than fifty years.

Armando Choy, Gustavo Chui, and Moisés Sío Wong, three young rebels of Chinese Cuban ancestry, became combatants in the clandestine struggle and 1956–58 revolutionary war that brought down the US-backed dictatorship of Fulgencio Batista and opened the door to socialist revolution in the Americas. Each, in the course of a lifetime of revolutionary action, became a general in the Revolutionary Armed Forces of Cuba. Through their stories the economic, social, and political forces that gave birth to the Cuban nation and still shape our epoch unfold.

We see how millions of ordinary human beings like them—the "men and women from nowhere" who the rulers cannot even see—simply refused to accept a future without dignity or hope, refused to settle for less than they dreamed of. They marched onto the stage of history and changed its course, becoming different human beings themselves in the process.

The suggestion for this book originally came to us from Harry Villegas, himself a brigadier general (now retired) of Cuba's Revolutionary Armed Forces as well as a Hero of the Republic of Cuba. He is known throughout the world as Pombo, the nom de guerre given him in 1965 by Cuban Argentine revolutionary leader Ernesto Che Guevara when together they fought at the side of the anti-imperialist forces in the Congo, and over the next two years in Bolivia as well.

In February 2002 Pathfinder editors had just completed work on *From the Escambray to the Congo: In the Whirlwind of the Cuban Revolution* by Víctor Dreke. The book had been well received at the Havana International Book Fair and in spirited meetings across the former province of Las Villas in central Cuba, organized in collaboration with the Association of Combatants of the Cuban Revolution. We were already far along in preparing two more titles related to the Cuban Revolution and its place in the world: *October 1962: The 'Missile' Crisis as Seen from Cuba* by Tomás Diez; and *Marianas in Combat*, the story of Cuba's highest-ranking female officer, Brigadier General Teté Puebla, and the Mariana Grajales Women's Platoon in Cuba's revolutionary war.

Planning ahead, Villegas invited us one morning to the national headquarters of the Association of Combatants of the Cuban Revolution, of which he was at that time the executive vice president, and introduced us to Armando Choy, Gustavo Chui, and Moisés Sío Wong. *Our History Is Still Being Written* is the product of the work that began that day.

■

The three young Chinese Cubans, of similar age, grew up in different parts of Cuba, under different class and social conditions. With each following his own path, all three came to the same revolutionary course of action. They threw themselves into the great proletarian battle that defined their generation—the struggle to overthrow the Batista tyranny and defend Cuba's sovereignty and independence against the onslaught of the imperialist empire to the north.

The significance and historical weight of Chinese immigration to Cuba starting in the mid-nineteenth century emerges from their accounts. In proportion to population, this immigration to Cuba was greater than anywhere else in the Americas, the United States included. In fact, thousands of Chinese laborers brought to build railroads in the US West later emigrated to Cuba in hopes of finding better conditions of life and work.

The lucrative trafficking in tens upon tens of thousands of Chinese peasants—their impressment, their death-ship transport to Cuba, their indentured labor on sugar plantations supplementing the dwindling supply of African slaves, and above all their resistance, struggles, and unblemished record of combat in Cuba's 1868–98 independence wars against Spain—all that is sketched here in broad outlines. It is a story largely unknown outside Cuba.

What is presented here, however, is not history alone. This is one of the indispensable strands of revolutionary Cuba today. From the pre-1959 racist oppression and super-exploitation of Chinese as well as black labor, to the measures taken by the popular revolutionary government headed by Fidel Castro to end this discrimination and combat its legacy, to the integration of Cubans of Chinese origin into every level of social and political life today, the story unfolds. As Sío Wong puts it so forcefully, the greatest measure taken against discrimination "was the revolution itself."

"The Chinese community here in Cuba is different from Peru, Brazil, Argentina, or Canada," he emphasizes. "And that difference is the triumph of a socialist revolution."

■

The revolutionary overthrow of the Batista dictatorship on January 1, 1959, was not the end of a story. It was the beginning. After taking power, the working people of Cuba began building a new society that posed an intolerable "affront" to the prerogatives of capital. For more than half a century they have defended that society built on new foundations, holding at bay the strongest imperialist power that will ever stalk the globe. In doing so the Cuban toilers and their government have become a beacon, and an ally, to those the world over seeking to learn how to fight to transform their lives—and how to fight to *win*.

Among the many responsibilities Choy, Chui, and Sío Wong have each shouldered over the years—within the Revolutionary Armed Forces as well as in government assignments and in the leadership of the Communist Party of Cuba—participation in Cuba's internationalist missions abroad stands out.

"Because our system is socialist in character and commitment," Choy explains, revolutionaries in Cuba have always sought to act "in the interests of the majority of humanity inhabiting planet earth—not on behalf of narrow individual interests, or even simply Cuba's national interests."

Each served in Angola at various times between 1975 and 1988, as Cuba responded to the request of the Angolan government, just gaining independence from Portugal, for aid to defeat an imperialist-backed invasion by the armed forces of South Africa's apartheid regime.

Chui helped establish Cuba's internationalist military aid missions in Nicaragua, Ethiopia, and Mozambique. Choy served as ambassador to Cape Verde from 1986 to 1992. Sío Wong in 2003 helped Venezuela's toilers in their efforts to establish and extend small-scale urban agriculture. From 1992 to 2010 he served as president of the Cuba-China Friendship Association.

The full story of Cuba's sixteen-year internationalist mission to Angola is still to be told. But the first-hand experiences and assessments offered here by each of these three generals provide insights into that important period in the history of Cuba and southern Africa not readily available elsewhere. The significance for Africa and the world of the March 1988 victory of the Cuban-Angolan-Namibian forces over the South African apartheid military in the battle known as Cuito Cuanavale is powerfully presented.

■

Our History Is Still Being Written—the title comes from Chui—captures the revolutionary perspective and ongoing intensity of work of the book's three protagonists. In the final section, "The Special Period and Beyond," each of them is looking to the future.

Choy speaks as the head of the massive, multifaceted, multiyear project to clean up Havana Bay, and to transform the infrastructure of the historic port of Havana.

Sío Wong describes the responsibilities he assumed in 1986 and shouldered for more than two decades as president of the National Institute of State Reserves. It is a body vital not only to the military defense of the revolution, but also to the Cuban government's ability to respond—in marked contrast, on every level, to the capitalist government of the United States—to the needs of the population in times of natural disaster such as the hurricanes that frequently strike the island with devastating ferocity.

Chui recounts the responsibilities of the Association of Combatants of the Cuban Revolution of which he was one of the founding leaders. The organization comprises some 300,000 Cubans with decades of experience as the backbone of the revolution—from cadres of the Rebel Army and clandestine struggle against Batista's tyranny, to young doctors and teachers completing internationalist missions around the world today. The association is responsible for a political education program that reaches into every school and neighborhood in the country.

As each of the three generals makes clear, the future will be written not *for* the working people of Cuba, but *by* them.

■

Our History Is Still Being Written, published simultaneously in Spanish and English, came together over a period of almost four years. It is the product of several rounds of interviews, some collective and some individual, that took place in 2002 and 2004, and were completed in 2005.

Arrin Hawkins, Martín Koppel, Luis Madrid, and Michael Taber each participated with me in one or more of the interviews that gave us this book. Production—from transcription and initial translation to composition, proofreading, preparation of the digital files for printing, and distribution—has been the work of more than 200 volunteers around the world who work collectively, organized by the Pathfinder Printing Project.

A special note of thanks is owed to the Biblioteca Nacional "José Martí" in Havana, whose archives encompass a valuable collection of materials related to Chinese immigration in Cuba. Aid from the library's staff was indispensable in locating and reproducing a number of the graphics that bring these pages to life.

Other historical photos and graphics were located with the help of Delfín Xiqués of *Granma*, Manuel Martínez of *Bohemia*, Milton Chee of San Francisco, California, and through the individual efforts of Generals Choy, Chui, and Sío Wong.

Iraida Aguirrechu of Editora Política, the publishing house of the Communist Party of Cuba, participated at each stage in all the interviews. Without her determination, diligence, concern for accuracy, and attention to detail, this book would not have seen the light of day.

Finally, and above all, our thanks go to Generals Armando Choy, Gustavo Chui, and Moisés Sío Wong for the many hours they each made available for the work necessary to bring this book to fruition.

We are confident it will be received with thanks by those to whom it is dedicated: the new generations of fighting "men and women from nowhere" now emerging around the world, for whom the example of Cuba's socialist revolution shows the way forward.

November 2005

Cuba

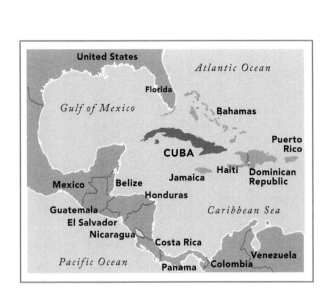

MAYABEQUE

HAVANA

Matanzas

VILLA CLARA

Guanajay

Artemisa

San José
de las Lajas

MATANZAS

Sagua
La Grande

PINAR DEL RÍO

ARTEMISA

BAY OF PIGS

Santa
Clara

Pinar del Río

Cienfuegos

Cabaigu

Fomento

Nueva Gerona

Playa Girón

CIENFUEGOS

ESCAMBRAY

Sancti
Spíritus

SANCTI SPÍRITUS

ISLE OF YOUTH

N

W   E

S

0   50   100   160 kilometers

0   50   100 miles

United States

Atlantic Ocean

Florida

Gulf of Mexico

Bahamas

Puerto
Rico

CUBA

Mexico

Belize

Jamaica

Haiti

Dominican
Republic

Guatemala

Honduras

Caribbean Sea

El Salvador

Nicaragua

Costa Rica

Venezuela

Pacific Ocean

Panama

Colombia

Chinese associations in Cuba, 1874–1959

Based on map by Fernando Ortiz Foundation

Top left: Armando Choy during interview, February 2004.

Top right: As ambassador to Cape Verde, 1991.

Bottom: As member of one of the revolutionary tribunals that tried hundreds of the Batista regime's murderers and torturers in the first months following January 1959 revolutionary victory. Next to Choy are Capt. Miguel Duque Estrada and Commander Víctor Bordón (far right).

Armando Choy

BORN 1934 IN FOMENTO, Las Villas province, Armando Choy Rodríguez moved to Santa Clara with his family when he was fourteen.

Following Fulgencio Batista's 1952 military coup, Choy joined the anti-Batista organization Joven Patria (Young Homeland). He was a founding member of the July 26 Movement in 1955. At the beginning of 1958 he became provincial leader of the organization's Student Front in Las Villas province and the head of two action and sabotage groups. On April 9, 1958, he led an armed group that participated in the nationwide general strike that day. As a result of his revolutionary activity he was arrested and jailed five times.

In May 1958 he joined a guerrilla unit of the July 26 Movement in the Escambray mountains led by Commander Víctor Bordón. When Rebel Army Column 8, led by Commander Ernesto Che Guevara, arrived in the Escambray in October, Bordón's unit became part of it. On December 26 of that year Guevara promoted Choy to captain, the second-highest rank in the Rebel Army. Choy took part in combat actions in Mordazo, Manacas, and Santo Domingo that culminated in the victorious battle for Santa Clara, the third most important city in Cuba.

Following the January 1, 1959, fall of the dictatorship,

Choy served on the revolutionary tribunals that tried war criminals of the Batista regime. In mid-1959, when the Rebel Army's Combat Tactical Forces were created in the east, center, and west of the country, he became deputy head of the central region's Infantry Regiment. In 1960 he headed the Revolutionary National Militia in Las Villas province, helping to organize the struggle against counterrevolutionary bands there.

In early 1961 Choy became payroll master of the newly formed Central Army. During the April 1961 US-backed mercenary invasion at the Bay of Pigs, which was defeated seventy-two hours later at Playa Girón, he was head of one of the units engaged in combat, the 345th Infantry Battalion, from what is today Sancti Spíritus province.

Later that year he was assigned to organize and command the infantry division of Sancti Spíritus and later that of Trinidad. Both participated in the campaign against counterrevolutionary bands in the Escambray mountains.

Promoted to commander in December 1962, Choy was transferred to the Anti-Aircraft Defense and Revolutionary Air Force (DAAFAR) in April 1963, and became head of the Antiaircraft Missile Defense Brigade of the Western Army. In 1973 he was named head of antiaircraft missile forces and deputy missile commander of DAAFAR. He was promoted to brigadier general in November 1976 and later to deputy head of the DAAFAR.

Choy participated in the internationalist mission in Angola from 1980 to 1982. Upon his return, he served in DAAFAR's leadership until December 1986, when he was named ambassador to the Republic of Cape Verde, a responsibility he held until 1992.

From 1992 until his retirement in 2015, he served as president of the State Working Group for the Cleanup, Preservation, Development, and Maintenance of Havana Bay and Its Tributary Basin. He organized the administration of the Port of Havana and served there as the representative of the Ministry of Transportation.

Choy retired from active duty in the Revolutionary Armed Forces in 1992. He is a founding member of the Communist Party of Cuba and of the Association of Combatants of the Cuban Revolution.

Top left: Gen. Gustavo Chui speaking to troops in Angola, December 1987.

Top right: During interview, February 2002.

Bottom: Chui, left, with Fidel Castro, on the occasion of Chui's promotion to brigadier general, 1980. Between them are Div. Gen. Francisco Cabrera and Brig. Gen. Línder Calzadilla.

Gustavo Chui

BORN 1938 IN SANTIAGO DE CUBA, Gustavo Chui Beltrán joined the revolutionary movement at age sixteen. He was active in the July 26 Movement's urban underground in Santiago during the first part of the revolutionary war.

In the spring of 1958 he joined the Rebel Army in the Sierra Maestra, where he was assigned to the Third Front under the command of Juan Almeida. He participated in a number of battles as a combatant in Column 3, under the command of Guillermo García. After the revolutionary victory of January 1, 1959, he took part in the Freedom Caravan from Santiago de Cuba to Havana.

On January 9, 1959, Chui was posted to the Managua military camp in Havana, under the orders of Commander Almeida. There he was assigned to an infantry battalion and then a tank company. In July 1959, he was sent to Belgium to study infantry armaments. Returning in September 1960, he assumed technical responsibility for the Department of War Matériel at Camp Managua. Later he served as armaments chief of the Revolutionary Air Force.

In April 1961, Chui was named head of armaments in Pinar del Río province, under Commander Ernesto Che Guevara. There he was in charge of arming the Revolutionary National Militias and army units that combated counterrevolutionary bands and fought at the Bay of Pigs.

The following year he became the Western Army's head of armaments.

In 1965 he was deputy head of the Armaments Subdirectorate of the Revolutionary Armed Forces (FAR). In 1968 he became head of the FAR's Armaments Directorate.

In September 1972 he was named second in command of the 10th Directorate of the FAR, the unit responsible for Cuba's internationalist military assistance. In December 1975, after the death in combat in Angola of Commander Raúl Díaz Argüelles, Chui replaced him as head of the 10th Directorate. Simultaneously he was assigned to head the staff of the Ministry of the Revolutionary Armed Forces' Special Command Post, assisting Commander in Chief Fidel Castro and Minister of the Revolutionary Armed Forces Raúl Castro in directing Cuba's internationalist mission in Angola.

In 1977 Chui was deputy head of the commission that organized Cuba's military aid to the government of Ethiopia. He also helped establish Cuban military missions in Mozambique and Nicaragua.

He was promoted to brigadier general in December 1980. In 1981 he was named head of the FAR's Cadres Directorate, in charge of assignment and supervision of the officers of the armed forces. From 1983 to 1986 he was deputy chief of the FAR's general staff.

In 1986, Chui was sent to Angola as deputy chief of staff of the military mission. In November 1987 he was assigned to head Operation 31st Anniversary of the Granma Landing, whose mission was to provide reinforcement for the battle of Cuito Cuanavale.

In December 1987, he was named head of the 90th Tank Brigade in Malanje. In March 1988, while leading an operation of this brigade in northern Angola, he was critically wounded and lost a leg after his vehicle hit an antitank mine.

In 1990, he joined the Association of Combatants of the Cuban Revolution when it was first organized in Pinar del Río as a pilot project. Since 1993, when it was officially founded as a national organization, until 2011, Chui headed the secretariat of finances and supplies as part of the association's national leadership. In 1998 Chui retired from active military duty.

Chui is a founding member of the Communist Party of Cuba. Since 2008, he has served as president of the Chung Wah Casino Federation, the umbrella organization of Chinese associations in Cuba.

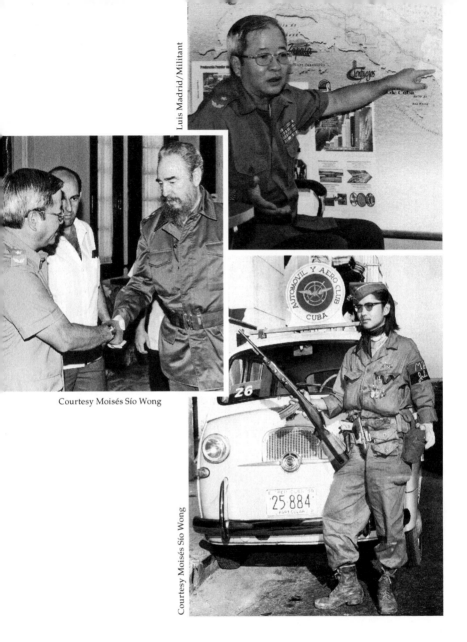

Luis Madrid/Militant

Courtesy Moisés Sío Wong

Courtesy Moisés Sío Wong

Top: Moisés Sío Wong during interview, August 2005.

Middle: Greeting Fidel Castro during luncheon at Havana embassy of People's Republic of China, March 1996.

Bottom: As member of Rebel Army Column 8, January 1959.

Moisés Sío Wong

BORN 1938 IN MATANZAS PROVINCE, Moisés Sío Wong moved with his family to Havana in 1947. He joined the fight against the Batista dictatorship as a high school student, participating in demonstrations and other protest actions and became a member of the July 26 Movement soon after its founding in 1955. Under the command of Gerardo Abreu (Fontán), he led its first Youth Brigade in Havana.

In 1957 he joined the Rebel Army in the Sierra Maestra, serving in the command post platoon of Column 1 led by Fidel Castro. He participated in the battles that defeated the Batista army's offensive in 1958. In August he was assigned to Column 8 led by Ernesto Che Guevara, and participated in the column's advance from the Sierra Maestra mountains to Las Villas province.

Following the January 1, 1959, revolutionary victory, Sío Wong was promoted to first lieutenant and became a founder of the Rebel Army's military police. During the US-organized invasion at the Bay of Pigs in April 1961, he was head of the 7th Infantry Division in Pinar del Río under the command of Guevara. A founder of the Western Army as first operations officer, Sío Wong subsequently worked in the Anti-Aircraft Defense and Revolutionary Air Force (DAAFAR), where his responsibilities included head of the Central Division. In

1965 he was named adjutant to Raúl Castro, minister of the Revolutionary Armed Forces, holding that responsibility for seven years.

In 1976 Sío Wong served as part of Cuba's internationalist military mission in Angola as head of logistics. In November of that year he was promoted to brigadier general. From 1982 to 1985 he headed the FAR's Cadres Directorate, in charge of assignment and supervision of the officers of the armed forces.

In 1986 he was named president of the National Institute of State Reserves (INRE), a responsibility he held until 2010.

A founding member of the Communist Party of Cuba, Sío Wong was president of the Cuba-China Friendship Association from 1992 to 2010.

As a member of the National Assembly of People's Power and its International Relations Commission, he was president of the Parliamentary Group for Friendship with China. In the early 1990s he was central to initiating the urban agriculture program that has expanded throughout Cuba. In 2003 he helped initiate a similar program in Venezuela.

Sío Wong was a founding member of the Association of Combatants of the Cuban Revolution. He retired from active military service in 1998 and returned to active duty in 2005, where he served until his death in 2010.

PART I

'The difference is a socialist revolution'

Chinese in Cuba

Bohemia

Members of Chinese New Democracy Alliance at million-strong General Assembly of the Cuban People, held in Havana September 2, 1960. The mass rally, organized in response to US efforts to line up Latin American governments against Cuba, approved a reply to Washington known as the First Declaration of Havana. Banner reads: "Resident Chinese support the Cuban Revolution and its leader, Fidel Castro!"

On September 28, 1960, Cuba became first country in Latin America to recognize the People's Republic of China, in defiance of Washington's efforts to isolate Beijing.

Three revolutionaries

MARY-ALICE WATERS: The three of you were each part of the generation of youth in Cuba whose struggle brought down the US-backed Batista dictatorship at the end of the 1950s and established the first government in the Americas that fights to advance the interests of the working classes. You yourselves were transformed by those struggles and the fight to consolidate and defend the "first free territory of the Americas."

How did you become cadres of the revolution? What was it like for each of you growing up in prerevolutionary Cuba? What discrimination did you face because of your Chinese ancestry? Why did you join the revolutionary movement?

ARMANDO CHOY

ARMANDO CHOY RODRÍGUEZ: I was born in 1934 in the town of Fomento, in what was then Las Villas province. I was one of four children, three girls and a boy.

The Fomento area was quite rich in agricultural and mineral resources, perhaps the richest in Cuba. There were two sugar mills. It was a major tobacco- and coffee-growing region, and still is. A lot of livestock too; cattle were taken to the cities for slaughter. And there were even some copper mines.

Fomento had a big Chinese community, a few of whom

were quite powerful economically. A number of the large businesses were owned by Chinese. My godfather, along with another Chinese man, owned Fomento's baseball stadium, for example. He also owned a number of stores and houses. After 1959 my godfather's property interests were adversely affected by the social measures of the revolution, and he left Cuba for the United States.

My father was born in China, coming to Cuba in 1918, I believe. He was brought over by his uncle, who owned a store in Palos, in Havana province, and had a lot of money.

My father is an unusual case. He came to Cuba, went back to China, and then returned again. Among the Chinese who emigrated to Cuba, this was very rare. Clearly he would not have been able to do this if his uncle hadn't been well-off.

At home, when I was growing up, we spoke only Spanish. My father used to say that you didn't learn to speak Chinese unless you studied it at school.

My mother, who wasn't Chinese, was a very hard-working Cuban woman. She was a fanatical supporter of Eduardo Chibás, leader of the Orthodox Party. My father, too, admired him. Every Sunday night at 8:00 P.M. my father would listen to Chibás's weekly radio broadcasts, which had begun to be aired in the late 1940s.

To give you an example of where my mother's sympathies lay: When I told her I was going off to join the armed struggle in the mountains to fight the Batista dictatorship, the only thing she said to me was "Be careful." Not that I shouldn't go, but "Be careful."

In 1948, when I was fourteen years old, my parents moved to Santa Clara, the capital of Las Villas province. Back then the current provinces of Sancti Spíritus, Cienfuegos, and Villa Clara were a single province. At that time in Fomento you could study up to the sixth grade, but no further. We moved

Armando Choy (left) working in his father's store in Santa Clara, 1952 or 1953.

Choy recalled an incident when a man walked in, crying. "He asked me to advance him a pound of corn meal on credit. It was all that his family would have had to eat that day. I gave it to him."

"He's not going to pay you," my father said.

"That doesn't matter," I replied.

"Do you know how much a pound of corn meal cost then? Seven cents. He didn't even have seven cents!"

That was one of many experiences that "convinced me of the injustice prevailing in Cuba before the triumph of the revolution."

to Santa Clara so I could continue my studies.

MARTÍN KOPPEL: What did your family do?

CHOY: My father was a merchant. At first he had a grocery store. Later he became a traveling salesman, representing various importing firms. After we moved to Santa Clara, he owned a small general store.

For five years I worked in this store during the day and studied accounting at night at the business school. Accounting! I wasn't especially interested in it. What I wanted to study was history. But my father, who was thinking about his business, said no.

An incident when I was working at my father's store still sticks in my memory. One day around noon, a man walked in. I knew him, since he always used to pass by the store. The man came in crying. He wasn't putting on an act. He asked me to sell him a pound of corn meal on credit. It was all that he, his wife, and his two children were going to eat that day for lunch, their main meal. He asked me to advance him a pound of corn meal. I gave it to him.

"He's not going to pay you for it," my father said.

"That doesn't matter," I replied.

Do you know how much a pound of corn meal cost then? Seven cents. He didn't even have seven cents!

I recall something else from my youth that had an impact on me.

I had gone back to Fomento, perhaps on vacation, I don't recall. A friend of mine lived there, the son of a fairly well-off Chinese man and a mother who was white. He had a girlfriend whose parents were of Spanish descent.

One night there was a party in town. I remember that as we approached the Spanish neighborhood—there was a Spanish neighborhood in all the towns—he said, "Let's go to the dance." I decided not to go along, since I never really liked dancing.

But when my friend and the girl tried to get in, they were turned away because he was Chinese. It was for whites only!

That act of discrimination convinced me of the injustice prevailing in Cuba before the triumph of the revolution.

Into the revolutionary struggle

WATERS: When did you get involved in the revolutionary struggle?

CHOY: As a student in Santa Clara. On the very day of Batista's coup d'état, March 10, 1952.

I opposed the coup and soon joined an anti-Batista organization. This was before the attack on the Moncada garrison.[1] In Santa Clara there were two revolutionary groups. One was called Acción Cívica Constitucional [Constitutional Civic Action] led by Osvaldo Herrera. And there was another group called Joven Patria [Young Homeland] led by Benigno Piñeiro, who later became a traitor. I joined Joven Patria.

I always say I'm a Fidelista going back to July 26, 1953. Because on that day, when the radio announced that Dr. Fidel Castro was the leader of the Moncada attack, I said, "That's the man we need to fight the dictatorship."

In the summer of 1955 Frank País, by then a national leader of the July 26 Movement from Santiago, came to Santa Clara to establish the organization there. I didn't meet him. But that's when the July 26 Movement was organized in the city, and the majority of us young people went over to it. The organization locally was led by Quintín Pino Machado. He was a great leader, who later became a political officer with us in the Revolutionary Armed Forces.

I was a student leader and helped organize action and sab-

---

1. For the Moncada attack and other historical events and figures referred to throughout the interview, see glossary starting on p. 189.

otage activities. I participated in student struggles and took part in street demonstrations, strikes, and other actions. I was arrested several times.

ARRIN HAWKINS: For what?

CHOY: From the moment I joined the July 26 Movement, I became more and more action-oriented—starting with the simplest tasks, such as painting slogans on walls against the Batista dictatorship and participating in student demonstrations. At the beginning these demonstrations were relatively peaceful. But later they usually ended up in fierce physical encounters with the army's Military Intelligence Service (SIM) and with the police. I also participated in sabotage actions, using Molotov cocktails and Brazilian grenades, although we could never get those grenades to explode.

As a result of these activities, I was jailed six times. Twice I was brought to trial before the Urgency Court.[2] I was acquitted both times.

At the beginning of 1958 I was named head of the July 26 Movement's Student Front in Las Villas province. That's what I was doing up to April 9, in addition to heading two action and sabotage units.

WATERS: April 9, 1958, is the day the July 26 Movement called a nationwide general strike against the dictatorship.[3] It failed utterly. What happened in Santa Clara that day? What were you doing?

2. See glossary, Urgency Courts.

3. See glossary, April 9 general strike. For accounts of the April 9 events by leaders of the July 26 Movement's urban underground, see Armando Hart, *Aldabonazo: Inside the Cuban Revolutionary Underground, 1952–58* (Pathfinder, 2004). The reorganization of the July 26 Movement following the April 9 events is described in the chapter "A Decisive Meeting" in Ernesto Che Guevara, *Episodes of the Cuban Revolutionary War, 1956–58* (Pathfinder, 1996).

CHOY: Groups of young workers and students were waiting to receive arms that morning, so that at the agreed-upon signal—which was to be the ringing of the bell of La Pastora Church at 11:00 AM—we would head out into the streets to support the strike. In fact only one group, that of the Condado neighborhood, received rifles. Another group, composed of students from the business high school and commanded by me, received four pistols.

Compañeros were supposed to ring the church bell, but they never did. The Condado group, together with ours, located in the La Pastora neighborhood, went out into the street anyway. The Condado group fought courageously against the dictatorship's army and police, and several experienced clandestine fighters—Antonio Aúcar Jiménez, David Díaz Guadarrama, and Héctor Martínez Valladares—were killed. Later on another of these valiant combatants, Eduardo "Bayoya" García, was captured and murdered by the tyranny's henchmen.

Since we never got the signal, the only thing our group of combatants from the business high school did was disarm a lone policeman.

It was lucky our compañeros didn't ring the church bell, however. Had we gone off to try to block the movement of the army and police with just five handguns—four pistols plus the revolver taken from the cop—we'd have been killed for sure. The disparity of weapons was too great. But I was young and didn't stop to think about things like that too much.

From that day on, I was totally underground.

At the end of April the movement transferred me to the city of Cienfuegos. While I was hiding out in Santa Clara, they told me that Aleida March—an outstanding fighter who joined the armed struggle in the mountains and later was married to Che

Guevara—would come see me on such and such a day. She
and I were comrades in the clandestine struggle then. So she
came and told me, "OK Choy, tomorrow someone will come
get you." I think the person's name was Morejón, a driver who
worked near my house and was in the July 26 Movement.
Two others were in Morejón's car, both from Sagua la
Grande on their way to Cienfuegos. One was Víctor Dreke.
The other was named Garrido, whose brother had been killed
in Sagua. Garrido was no good—he was a coward and a
half—and he later turned traitor. Dreke, however, was quite
a good combatant and compañero, as we know.[4]

In Cienfuegos they checked us into a clinic as patients. I
recall that a revolutionary nurse named Víctor gave me the
name Armando Pi.

"Why are you giving me a Spaniard's name?" I asked him.
"Give me a Chinese last name. Because they're going to find
me out with that one."

"Look, if they figure out who you are, they'll kill you anyway," Víctor told me. "So keep the name we gave you."

From Cienfuegos I went up to the mountains.

Taking up arms

KOPPEL: What happened after you got there?

CHOY: A front of the July 26 Movement, led by Commander
Víctor Bordón, had recently been opened in the Escambray
mountains. I became a member of this guerrilla unit on May 9,
1958. I was the nineteenth member. I joined as a simple combatant and was promoted to lieutenant by Bordón in August.

This guerrilla column is a little-known chapter of the July

4. For Dreke's own account of this episode and much more, see *From
the Escambray to the Congo: In the Whirlwind of the Cuban Revolution*
(Pathfinder, 2002).

26 Movement in Las Villas. We had six combat engagements before being integrated into the column led by Commander Che Guevara in October 1958. In fact, my first San Cristóbal automatic rifle was seized by us during an ambush we carried out in the Mandulo region, located in what's today the province of Cienfuegos.

We had serious frictions with another organization there called the Second National Front of the Escambray, which had betrayed the Revolutionary Directorate and split from it. The majority of its soldiers were OK. But its main officers were bandits, and later, after 1959, they also became counterrevolutionaries. That's the reality, as events showed. They wound up being part of imperialism's forces.

In October 1958 we received orders to march eastward through the mountains to join up with Che, whose column had just arrived after a difficult trek from the Sierra Maestra.[5] Our march to meet them lasted about two days. It had to be undertaken very carefully, since we thought we were going to have a confrontation with the Second Front of the Escambray. Fortunately there was no such encounter, as it would have been painful to suffer deaths from a struggle within the ranks of revolutionary combatants. I was named second in command of the forward detachment, which had sixty-five combatants under Captain Cente—Edelberto González.

5. For an account of the Rebel Army columns led by Che Guevara and Camilo Cienfuegos that marched from the Sierra Maestra in eastern Cuba to Las Villas province in the center of the island during September–October 1958—in what is known in Cuba as the "invasion"—see Guevara, *Episodes of the Cuban Revolutionary War, 1956–58*, "From Batista's Final Offensive to the Battle of Santa Clara," and "The Las Villas Campaign, September–December 1958." Also Luis Alfonso Zayas, *Soldier of the Revolution: From the Cane Fields of Oriente to General of the Revolutionary Armed Forces* (Pathfinder, 2011).

When we got to an area called Las Piñas, Che spoke to us. That's when we began joint operations.

In December Che promoted me to captain and assigned me a platoon of twenty-six new combatants. As a member of Che's column, I participated in a number of battles that contributed to the Rebel Army's liberation of Las Villas province. That offensive culminated in the battle for Santa Clara, which ended on January 1, 1959, when Batista fled.

I was then ordered to be part of the advance on Havana with Bordón's column, reinforcing Column 2, under the command of Camilo Cienfuegos. On January 2 we reached Matanzas and took the surrender of the army's regiment there. Later that day we reached Havana and accepted the surrender of Camp Columbia, the old army's main military camp. The following day I was reassigned to Che's column.

WATERS: Did the fact that you are of Chinese descent have an impact on the development of your revolutionary consciousness?

CHOY: Not really. Clearly, being the son of a Chinese parent fostered a special warmth toward China, and I greatly admire that country and its heroic and selfless people. But I joined the movement as a Cuban. I thought like a Cuban, not like someone from China.

I was coordinator for the July 26 Movement's Student Front in the old province of Las Villas. The leading Cubans from the other high schools accepted me as any other Cuban. Within the movement there was no discrimination.

GUSTAVO CHUI

WATERS: General Chui, you grew up in Santiago de Cuba, in eastern Cuba. Was your family background similar to Choy's?

GUSTAVO CHUI BELTRÁN: No, it was quite different. In Santiago there was a Chinatown composed of a fair number of Chinese and their descendants, although it was smaller than Havana's.

My father, José Chui, got together with my mother, Ana Hilda Beltrán, who was poor and black. After I was born there was a conflict between the two, primarily because my father's closest compatriots were opposed to the marriage owing to the racial prejudices of the time. This was especially true of my father's main business partner, with whom he owned a grocery store. My father and his partner went to court to change my birth certificate. I had been born in 1938, but they put down I'd been born two years earlier, in order to take away my mother's parental rights. They paid off a lawyer to do this. My mother, a poor black woman, lacked the economic means to prevent it. Because of this, I remained under my father's care. I learned all this only when I was older, after my mother had died.

At that time we lived in the grocery store, together with the other Chinese who worked there. I spent most of my time in the backyard. I never went out and had nothing to do with other children in the neighborhood. As a result I spoke Cantonese only, not Spanish. One reason for all this was to keep me away from my mother.

We lived in the neighborhood of Los Olmos in Santiago de Cuba, through which General Wood Street runs (now it's René Ramos Latour Street). Our house was across the street from the Rubio canvas shoe factory (today it's a textile mill).

When I was about five years old, they let me go out into the neighborhood for the first time, and I began playing with other children my age. But the other kids couldn't understand me, and I couldn't understand them. They'd speak to me in Spanish and I'd answer in Chinese. Everyone would laugh at me. So I found a way to learn Spanish and started forgetting Chinese. Even when my father spoke to me in Chinese, I'd answer him in Spanish.

Among the Chinese I was called Conchan. So the children called me that too. That's what most of my relatives and friends in Santiago de Cuba still call me.

My father had no more children in Cuba. Before he came over from China, he'd had a few children, but I don't know anything about them. That's not the case with my mother. She had another son, my brother Jorge Luis, who lives in Santiago de Cuba.

My father's main partner, Arsenio Hung, had a large family, and I was counted as the oldest son, since I helped care for his children for a period of time. What's more, owing to my father's changes of jobs, at times I lived with the families of other Chinese who were partners of his. During my childhood I had three foster mothers, and I ended up with a large number of foster brothers and sisters.

My father was a merchant, as were most Chinese who lived in Santiago. The most common businesses were stores, small restaurants, bakeries, laundries, bars, vegetable stands, things like that.

My father and Arsenio had a grocery store that went bankrupt. Later they bought a bakery in the Sierra Maestra, in a place called San José de Aserradero, but it too failed.

My father and I had to move to Havana, this time at the urging of my cousin Rafael Wong, who owned a candy shop on Manrique Street, where today there's a day-care center. After my cousin sold the candy shop, he bought a bar on San Rafael Street. Later he sold the bar and bought the Chan Li Po cafeteria on Virtudes Street. For two years I lived with this family, under the care of Barbarita, one of my foster mothers.

In Havana I studied at the Sara Madera school and later in

the Campos school, both in the Lawton neighborhood, where my father's cousin and his family lived.

WATERS: Did you maintain any contact with your mother while you were growing up?

CHUI: I learned afterward that she used to watch me from afar, since she feared running into my Chinese family, who had threatened her and told her to keep away from me.

I was living in Havana in 1945, when the Second World War ended. I remember this because of the little tune they used to sing back then: "Bim bim, there goes Berlin. Bam bam, there goes Japan." Arsenio asked my father to return to Santiago, since he had a new bakery, La Cubanita, in the Sueño neighborhood; it still exists. By then Arsenio was married and had a number of small children. That's where I lived for some ten years. It was one of the more stable periods I knew.

My father and his partner sold this bakery and bought another one, called Las Américas, located in the same neighborhood, and it too is still there. I began to go to the San Lucas Episcopal School in front of Maceo Stadium, where I studied until seventh grade.

This buying and selling of bakeries turned out to be quite frequent for my father and Arsenio Hung. Because of this, we covered a lot of ground in Santiago. Among the bakeries I can point to are La Moderna, in the Sorribe neighborhood, and Nueva China, close to the Spanish neighborhood in Alto de Quinteros.

July 26 Movement cadre

HAWKINS: What attracted you to the revolutionary movement?

CHUI: My father and his Chinese partners lived relatively comfortably, and I didn't experience hard times. But I always sensed the social and political atmosphere around me in the various neighborhoods where I lived.

Events such as the 1952 coup d'état by dictator Fulgencio Batista shook the people, especially the youth. After the attack on the Moncada garrison, we were becoming more and more conscious of the unjust character of that merciless regime.

At the beginning of 1957 I joined the July 26 Movement. I became part of a cell led by Miguel Mariano Martínez Hierrezuelo, a revolutionary fighter who later became a Rebel Army captain.

Initially I participated in action and sabotage activities. The first missions consisted of obtaining food and medicine for the revolutionaries who were being hidden or were wounded. Later I distributed propaganda, placed homemade bombs, and engaged in other activities that expressed our spirit of rebellion, our willingness to fight to overthrow the tyranny. I carried out these types of missions until shortly before the strike of April 9, 1958. After that I went up to the Sierra Maestra, where I joined the "Mario Muñoz Monroy" Third Front, led by Commander Juan Almeida Bosque.

I should stress that it was one of my foster mothers, Lidia Wanton, who took me there. She was married to Antonio Fong, one of my father's Chinese friends, and they had a small farm in the Sierra Maestra called El Lucero. At the insistence of her son, who was already a member of the Third Front, she came to Santiago to get me.

When I reached the Sierra, I went before Captain Enrique López in La Anita camp. I became part of the troops under the command of Lieutenant Idelgarde Rivaflecha, who was known as Jabao Cuchillo. After the Batista army's summer

1958 offensive was over,[6] I became part of the "Santiago de Cuba" Column 3, led by Commander Guillermo García.

As a member of this column I participated in a number of battles and skirmishes, among them the capture of Palma Soriano, which initiated the preparations for the planned attack on Santiago de Cuba. On January 1, 1959, as the column was heading off toward its objective—while we were in the village of Escandel—we learned that the army of the tyranny had surrendered.

Now victorious, we entered Santiago de Cuba, and on the night of January 1 my platoon was assigned to guard Céspedes Park. It was from there that the commander in chief spoke to the people of Santiago de Cuba and the entire nation.

Then the Liberty Caravan left en route to Havana, with Fidel in the lead.[7]

6. Taking advantage of the momentum gained from the collapse of the April 9, 1958, strike, the Batista army sent 10,000 troops into the Sierra Maestra, in an attempt to annihilate the revolutionary forces. The Rebel Army fighters, who numbered 300 in late May, when the offensive began, with only 200 usable rifles, withstood, and by late July crushed, this effort.

    For accounts of this period, see Guevara, *Episodes of the Cuban Revolutionary War*, "From Batista's Final Offensive to the Battle of Santa Clara," and Hart, *Aldabonazo: Inside the Cuban Revolutionary Underground*. See also Fidel Castro, *From the Sierra Maestra to Santiago de Cuba: Strategic Counteroffensive* (in Spanish; Havana: Office of Publications of the Council of State, 2010).

    For accounts of the revolutionary underground in Santiago, see *Aldabonazo* by Armando Hart, and Vilma Espín and Asela de los Santos in *Women in Cuba: The Making of a Revolution within the Revolution* (Pathfinder, 2012).

7. From January 2 to January 8, 1959, Fidel Castro led a victorious Rebel Army column from the Sierra Maestra to Havana. The Freedom Caravan, as it was known, was greeted by masses of Cubans in cities and towns across the island who turned out to meet the "men from Moncada."

MOISÉS SÍO WONG

WATERS: General Sío Wong, you grew up in Havana, and I take it your family background was different from that of Generals Choy and Chui. Is this right?

MOISÉS SÍO WONG: Yes. My father arrived in Cuba in 1895. He came from China with his first wife. He had his first child in China—that is, my oldest brother. My father left my brother there with the boy's grandmother, and he came here to Cuba with his wife.

WATERS: In what circumstances?

SÍO WONG: He simply got the money together, bought the ticket, and came. He settled in Matanzas province, where there was a big Chinese community. He had a little grocery store in a small village in the countryside called San Pedro de Mayabón, in Los Árabos municipality.

My father had five children with his first wife. One in China and four here. His wife died, leaving him a widower. Among the peasants it was common to say, "Send the man a wife." So he sent off for another one, who was to be my mother. She was fifteen when she arrived. At the time, my father's children were fourteen, thirteen, twelve, and eleven. So my mother was only a year older than the eldest child she was caring for.

My mother should have gotten a medal. A heroine. She bore him nine children. In addition, she cared for four of the five children by my father's first marriage. When I was born in 1938, there were already eleven children in the household. I was number twelve.

During the first years of my life, we lived in San Pedro de Mayabón. It was a very small village, mostly peasants. I didn't go to school, but I did learn to read and write at home. My older sister Angelita, who'd attended school, taught me. I also learned arithmetic there—addition and subtraction.

At home we mainly spoke Chinese. But I learned Spanish too. Because even though I didn't go to a Cuban school at the time, many of the children I played with were not Chinese. As I grew older, I began forgetting Chinese, since I didn't use it much.

In 1947, when I was nine, my father suffered a stroke and became an invalid. The family moved here to Havana to better care for him.

My brother-in-law, who was Chinese, was very rich. He and my sister Isabel married in 1942 or 1943. I remember the huge wedding they had. I'd never seen anything like it. Chinese from all over Cuba came. Big trucks from Havana loaded down with beer, cake, sweets, and other delicacies. The wedding cake had seven layers. I was only a child, but I still remember that. This gentleman—my sister's husband—was the secretary of the Kuomintang in Cuba, the Chinese Nationalist Party, Chiang Kai-shek's party. He was a big businessman, with lots of money.

My brother-in-law opened a restaurant here in Havana, on San Lázaro and Crespo streets, a bar and restaurant where all my brothers and sisters worked. We got paid practically nothing.

At the time the minimum wage was 60 pesos a month. My brother later told me how my brother-in-law cooked the books to make it appear we were being paid 60 pesos. But he'd pay the oldest ones 45 at most. Sometimes even 30. And he didn't pay the children anything. He'd give us 20 centavos to go to the movies on Sunday. That was it.

I used to think my brother owned the bar, but it was my brother-in-law's and he was exploiting the entire family.

I found this out after returning from the revolutionary war. "Benito's been exploiting us," I told my mother.

"No," she replied. "We should thank him for putting up the money, setting up the business, and giving us work."

That was one way of looking at it, right? That he helped out our family by setting up the business. The other view—my view—was that we were being exploited. My brothers and sisters did the work and he got the profits. But I didn't fully understand "the exploitation of man by man" until after the triumph of the revolution.

After we came to Havana, I completed elementary school in two years. I already knew how to read and write. They gave me a test and put me in third grade. During summer vacation my sister got me a tutor and I jumped ahead to sixth grade. During other vacations the same tutor coached me, and I passed an exam to enter high school. That's how I completed elementary school in two years. We had to change my birth certificate to make me a year older, since you had to be twelve to get into high school and I was only eleven.

I spent a year in a private school, and then in 1951 I began attending Institute of Secondary Studies Number 1 in Havana. That's where I was when Batista carried out his coup on March 10, 1952.

Joining the revolutionary movement

KOPPEL: How did you come to join the revolutionary movement?

SÍO WONG: In Cuba students have always been in the vanguard of revolutionary struggles. On March 10 students at the University of Havana, led by young people like Fidel Castro and José Antonio Echeverría, vigorously protested the coup. That's how the struggle against the dictatorship began.

There was a strong student movement at the Institute of Secondary Studies, which had close ties to students at the University of Havana. A group of students at the high school quickly won me over. I didn't know anything about politics. I was very young. But it was there, as a student, that I began to express my feelings of discontent. Together with some other young people, we became active in the student struggle.

We began participating in demonstrations against the dictatorship together with students at the University of Havana. After the Moncada attack of July 26, 1953, these ties were even closer.

Historically, the University of Havana had played a prominent role in the struggles for independence, as well as during the 1933 revolution.[8] Fidel and many other leaders came out of the battles at the university.

Prior to July 26 we had ties to the left wing of the Orthodox Party—which is what Fidel belonged to at the time. That's where I got to know a group of revolutionaries that included Ñico López and Enio Leyva, and where I was recruited.

A group of us young people who lived in the Punta neighborhood organized a series of talks that we called "civic talks." Ñico López, who later participated in the Moncada assault and was killed following the *Granma* landing, would speak. Ñico was a worker, tall and skinny, very poor and modest. The talks presented a revolutionary political perspective. They were held at the Orthodox Party office, at 109 Prado, on the tree-lined promenade in Havana. As I said, the July 26 Movement didn't yet exist. At that time there was a left-wing group in the Orthodox Party led by Fidel and some young people, including Ñico López, Juan Manuel Márquez, Enio Leyva, and René Rodríguez.

After the attack on Moncada, the July 26 Movement was founded in 1955 and we joined it. Here in Havana the July 26 Movement Youth Brigades were formed, made up largely of

8. See glossary, Revolution of 1933.

students and young workers. They were headed by Gerardo Abreu (Fontán), an outstanding revolutionary with great organizational capability. He was an honest, straightforward, and selfless compañero who was black. The youth brigades devoted themselves primarily to propaganda, painting slogans on walls, breaking display windows, throwing Molotov cocktails, small sabotage actions like that. Fontán named me head of the first youth brigade, created in the La Punta neighborhood.

By mid-1957 there was intense repression here in Havana, and it was decided I should go up to the Sierra Maestra. I headed off on July 4, Independence Day in the United States. I remember passing by a television on the street broadcasting a ceremony in which the US national anthem was being played.

I first went to Bayamo and waited there a few months, from July to November, before I received authorization to go up. In the meantime, I was underground, pretending to be the nephew of a Chinese man who owned a laundry there.

Finally, at the end of November 1957, I joined Fidel's column.

Member of Rebel Army

WATERS: What happened when you got to the Sierra?

SÍO WONG: The guerrilla unit was going through a critical juncture at that time.

The movement had gotten me a uniform, boots, a hammock, everything but a weapon. But I went up with three compañeros from Manzanillo—young peasants—who had nothing at all. They too were trying to join the Rebel Army, but they weren't bringing any food supplies or clothing.

I had a letter with me. It wasn't from Fontán, my immediate superior—he was the one I should have gotten a letter from. Instead, the letter was from one of the members of the *Granma* expedition. This compañero had come down from the mountains ill, and we had hidden him in a house. To us he was a god, a hero.

"Don't worry about a thing," the guy said. "I'll give you a letter to Fidel, and you won't have any problems." So he wrote me a letter of introduction to Fidel: "I send you Sío Wong, who's on the run owing to his revolutionary activities, and so on and so forth. Signed So-and-So." With that letter in hand, I thought I'd have no big problem.

It was difficult for me to make it up to the Sierra Maestra. I had been raised here in the city. I was a student. In addition, I was recovering from a fever, and I'd been very weak for three or four days. When I climbed the first hill, I fainted. The guide wanted to leave me behind but I told him, "If you leave me behind, I'm going to write to Fidel and they'll have you shot. You must take me up to the mountains."

So he borrowed a horse from a peasant woman, a widow who lived nearby. He put me on the horse, and that's how I reached the Sierra Maestra.

As we were arriving at Fidel's command post, I heard a compañero yell out, "Hey Fidel, even the Chinese are here!" That was my greeting.

They went inside a little house and gave Fidel my letter. I had always imagined that the compañeros would greet me with open arms.

"So, you're all on the run as a result of your work in the clandestine struggle?" Fidel said when he came out. "Where are you all from?"

The other guys said, "No, we're from somewhere different than he is, from Calicito. We've only burned a few cane fields."

At that very moment Fidel had a platoon in the same area burning cane fields. "So you're the ones who burned the Calicito cane fields?" he said. "Then why do I have Captain Basante there with a platoon?"

I don't know, it's possible these guys really had burned some sugarcane. But Fidel did have a platoon in that area carrying out this specific mission, burning cane in that area.

Then he turned to me: "And you? So you're the one sent to me by So-and-So?"

"Yes, commander."

"He obviously thinks he's a hero. He must be having the time of his life with the story of being part of the *Granma* expedition, instead of being here with us."

Then Fidel said, "Do you think this is an embassy? You do any little thing and then take sanctuary here? You didn't bring weapons, you didn't bring uniforms, you didn't bring boots, you didn't bring food, you didn't bring anything."

"Crescencio!" he yelled out. Crescencio Pérez, a peasant, was part of the rear guard. "Crescencio, lock them up for three days, with nothing but rice to eat."

I really felt terrible. Flabbergasted. I was convinced they'd receive me with open arms, and the opposite turned out to be the case.

The next day we were down at the river and Fidel came by. He apologized. "Please forgive me for the way I treated you yesterday, but this guy So-and-So really did a lousy thing. I gave him a direct order and he disobeyed. We face a critical situation with food, with clothes, with weapons. We don't have any weapons. If you want, you can all go back. When things get better, you can return."

"Commander, I can't go back to Havana," I said. "They're after me there."

The other three guys left, but I stayed. I remained in Column 1 led by Fidel and was eventually assigned to his command post in La Plata. I remained there until the Batista army's summer offensive began in 1958.

A clandestine mission

WATERS: While you were at the command post you were assigned a mission that required a clandestine trip back to Havana, right?

SÍO WONG: Yes. At the end of January 1958, Fidel was preparing to send someone to go find Fontán—Gerardo Abreu—to get him out of Havana, where he was in imminent danger, and bring him to the Sierra. Since I was from Havana, compañero René Rodríguez, one of the *Granma* expeditionaries, suggested to Fidel that I go. That was right around the time of the second battle of Pino del Agua, and I was unable to leave right then. The battle occurred on February 4 or 5, and on February 7 news reached us that Fontán had been murdered.

Fontán was a leader of the July 26 Movement Youth Brigades, very courageous, with great integrity, an extraordinary compañero. He knew the entire organization in Havana, but Batista's men were unable to get him to reveal a single piece of information, even though they tortured him savagely.

For me the news was doubly painful, because Fontán had been my first leader inside the movement. He had always exemplified for me what a revolutionary is. Plus I knew Fidel had been planning to send me to get him.

A few days later, I was given the mission of going to Havana to find Sergio González, who we all knew as El Curita—"the little priest." He was head of action and sabotage here in the capital. He too was very much on the run.

During those days new columns led by Raúl Castro and Juan Almeida were being organized to leave the Sierra and open the Second and Third Fronts. So it wasn't until March 10 that I could leave. I recall that I took advantage of Batista's celebrations of the anniversary of his coup to come down from the Sierra, go to Bayamo, make contacts, and then reach Havana.

I met El Curita in a park in the Víbora neighborhood of Havana at night, in front of the Mónaco movie theater. I'll never forget that meeting. I relayed Fidel's order to come back with me to the Sierra, since they were after him.

"Tell Fidel to forgive me for not obeying his order," Sergio González told me. "But as head of action and sabotage in such a complex situation, I can't go and abandon my men. I'm sure he'll understand. I'm grateful nevertheless for his concern for my safety."

There was no way he'd be convinced.

The meeting with Sergio González was on March 13, and I must have left Havana around March 14. When I informed Fidel that I had been unable to fulfill the mission, he was very sad, since he knew they were going to kill El Curita. And on March 19 they did. These were brave, proven, very valuable cadres who Fidel wanted to prevent from being killed.

Fidel knew the clandestine struggle in the city was very difficult. Fontán had been the victim of an informer. This person kept passing by, escorted by police in a patrol car, until he spotted Fontán in the street one day. That was how Fontán was nabbed.

I always give these cases as examples of how Fidel looked after the cadres, after the men, when he was leading a battle. He showed his concern for them and for having the fewest possible losses. But it's also an example of how these cadres assumed their responsibilities.

Fontán knew he was being hotly pursued. In fact, Fontán was the one who sent me to the Sierra. "They're close on your trail," he told me. "You have to go." Yet he himself remained in Havana. The same with El Curita, who also stayed, despite the order from Fidel. It showed their sense of responsibility. That was true for many others as well, starting with Fidel. There's a letter to Fidel written by the combatants in the Sierra, asking him not to participate directly in combat. Because there was a period when he took a lot of risks.[9]

As far as I'm concerned, the most difficult struggle was the clandestine struggle in the city. In the city the enemy has all the advantages. Unlike the mountains, where the guerrilla has the advantage. He's the one who sets the ambushes. But in the city, the enemy has the advantage. And Havana was the most difficult place of all.

In Che's column

KOPPEL: You mentioned the Batista army's offensive in the Sierra Maestra during the summer of 1958. What were you doing during those months?

SÍO WONG: I was with Fidel during the first part of the offensive. He then sent me with a mine—an unexploded 100-pound bomb dropped by an enemy plane, which we had converted into a mine—to hold back the enemy reinforcements that had landed to the south of the Sierra Maestra, near Palma Mocha. An elite enemy unit known as the Swift Battalion, under the command of Major Quevedo, was surrounded in El Jigüe, and Batista was sending reinforcements to break the siege. So Fidel sent me with a squad from Che's column to join Captain Ramón Paz's platoon.

In fact the enemy reinforcements didn't get there, since they were driven back by Captain Andrés Cuevas's platoon in a decisive battle in which this courageous officer was killed.

I spent the rest of the offensive with that squad, participat-

9. This letter can be found in Guevara, *Episodes of the Cuban Revolutionary War*, in the chapter "The Second Battle of Pino del Agua."

ing in a number of battles, including the battle of El Jigüe, which was led personally by Fidel.[10] I also took part in the battle of Casa de Piedra, Providencia, where Captain Ramón Paz was killed, and at Joval, where Commander René Ramos Latour (Daniel) died. When the offensive was over, I remained in Che's column.

In late August, Fidel designated Che and Camilo to organize two new columns. Che's column, "Ciro Redondo" Column 8, was to proceed toward the center of the country. Camilo's column, "Antonio Maceo" Column 2, had the mission of reaching Pinar del Río, the westernmost province.[11]

The choice of these two was a masterful decision by Fidel because of the qualities of both leaders. Che described Camilo as a tremendously creative combatant, a born guerrilla leader. The troops Camilo commanded had been in the plains of Bayamo, in Oriente, for several months, operating against the dictatorship's army. They had experience fighting in the plains. The rest of us had no experience fighting in the plains—all our combat had been in the mountains. Camilo's troops—the majority of the more than 90 combatants who set out—were veterans, with automatic weapons. That's why Camilo was given this mission.

As for Che's column of some 140 men, it was armed with weapons we had been able to assemble. The column included a group of officers and platoon and squad leaders who had served in the Sierra Maestra. But a large part of the column had just been through the School of Recruits in Minas del

10. The battle of El Jigüe, July 11–20, 1958, was a decisive Rebel Army victory that sealed the defeat of the government's offensive in the Sierra Maestra.

11. In October Fidel Castro ordered Column 2 to remain in Las Villas province and operate in coordination with Column 8.

Frío.[12] They were green. They had no combat experience.

I was in the forward detachment. Our platoon, which was made up of the most experienced combatants, had automatic weapons. I was in the second squad.

Before we left, Che got everyone together and explained the mission. Even if only a single combatant were left, Che said, he had to reach the destination and carry out the mission Fidel had given us.

I think Fidel chose Che to organize the struggle in the central part of the island for two reasons. First, because of the importance of that area. To be able to cut the dictatorship's forces in two. Second, because in Las Villas province there were troops from four different organizations: the July 26 Movement, led by Víctor Bordón; the Revolutionary Directorate, which was the student group, led by Faure Chomón; the Popular Socialist Party, which had a unit in the northern part of the province led by Félix Torres; and the Second National Front of the Escambray, which had split from the Revolutionary Directorate and had ties to the Authentic Organization.

Fidel's objective was to unify these groups and cut the island in two. Because of his political abilities, Che was one of those capable of doing this. Che combined an outstanding mind with the qualities of a man of action. He was a combatant and a thinker.

The advance into central Cuba took place under very difficult conditions. It took us forty-five days to reach the Escambray. Eleven compañeros just couldn't keep up physically and left the unit halfway through the march. Some of them were

12. In April 1958 Che Guevara helped establish a Rebel Army school for recruits at Minas del Frío in the Sierra Maestra. Participants received military training as well as literacy classes and political instruction.

murdered by the dictatorship.

Our feet were all chewed up not just from marching 500 kilometers, but also because we had to go through swamps, crossing the southern part of Camagüey province. It wasn't possible to use horses, cars, or anything else. We were on the move through very difficult conditions. In the mountains guerrillas have the advantage, but on the plains the enemy does, since he can move easily. And the enemy knew this terrain.

Whenever I felt I couldn't take any more, I'd look over at Che, who had used up the medication in his asthma inhaler. I'd see this Argentine guy with asthma who was willing to die for Cuba. If he could do it, how could I not do it? This gave me strength to keep going. I needed help from the other compañeros too, since sometimes I couldn't even lift my rifle, the lightweight M-1 carbine I was carrying. I'd grown up in the city and weighed less than 100 pounds.

Under these conditions we reached the Escambray in October 1958.

HAWKINS: What happened when you got there?

SÍO WONG: The first thing was that we bumped up against the forces of the Second National Front of the Escambray under the command of Jesús Carreras. We encountered a sign along the route into the mountains: "Troops from organizations other than the Second Front of the Escambray are not allowed here." It was signed by Carreras.

This organization had a provocative attitude, and they knew our column was coming.

Víctor Bordón had previously sent two officers to meet up with us. They'd guided us during the last part of the journey and had told us about the situation created by the Second Front.

Che succeeded in uniting the forces of the Revolutionary

Directorate, the July 26 Movement, and the PSP. A pact was signed with the Directorate—the Pedrero Pact—in which their troops united under Che's command, combining their actions. A little later the PSP signed on too. The Second Front of the Escambray didn't sign the pact.

Virtually without rest after the long trip, Che attacked several small garrisons in the foothills of the mountains, such as Güinía de Miranda, Banao, and Caracusey.

Güinía de Miranda was the first battle after we arrived. We attacked a small army garrison of 40 men. We attacked around 5:00 AM and the battle had to end before dawn. Otherwise enemy planes would have gotten us.

On the march from the Sierra Maestra, we'd brought along a bazooka that had been seized during the army's summer offensive. But the compañero assigned didn't really know how to shoot it. So when the battle began, his first shot flew over the garrison. The second one fell short.

Che came over. "Hey *chico*, what are you doing?" Che grabbed the bazooka, stood in front of the garrison, and fired. The shot went straight through a window and into the building. They surrendered on the spot.

During the weeks that followed, Batista's army launched an offensive in the Escambray, which was repelled, and our troops passed over to what became the final offensive.

One of the toughest battles occurred in Fomento, Choy's hometown. It was December 16, the first time we had assaulted an army garrison of that size in an urban area. We were attacked from the air during this three-day battle. After the enemy surrendered, we went on to liberate other cities including Cabaiguán, Placetas, Sancti Spíritus, Remedios, and Caibarién.

I remember an incident from the battle of Cabaiguán.

The forward platoon I was in, crossing through backyards,

had managed to get right up to the enemy garrison, just across the street. I went to inform Che that we'd taken up this very advantageous position. To get there, you had to jump from a roof onto a wall, and then into a backyard. But it was 4:00 in the morning and dark. Che took a false step and fell, breaking his arm.

"What happened to the m-1?" Those were the first words out of Che's mouth. He's just broken his arm and he's asking about the rifle he was carrying!

The fighting culminated in the battle of Santa Clara. On January 1, 1959, we won that battle, Batista fled the island, and we headed for Havana.[13]

I thought the war was over. I went through something similar to what López Cuba describes in *Making History*.[14] I'd left high school. I needed only two classes to get my diploma. So I went up to Che:

"OK, Che, the war's over. I want to become an electrical engineer."

"You're leaving *now*?" Che responded. "Don't be a jerk. Now the revolution begins."

WATERS: So you continued under Che's command?

SÍO WONG: I was promoted to first lieutenant in early January 1959 and assigned to the military police, organized out of the La Cabaña fortress in Havana. That was Che's command post. The military police were in charge of overseeing military discipline. I also took night classes at the Institute of Secondary Studies. But I'd been out of school for four years and found it very hard to study. Plus, there were all

13. See Guevara, *Episodes of the Cuban Revolutionary War*, "The Las Villas campaign, September–December 1958."

14. Mary-Alice Waters, ed., *Making History: Interviews with Four Generals of Cuba's Revolutionary Armed Forces* (Pathfinder, 1999).

the responsibilities of the Rebel Army.

Some months later Jorge Ricardo Masetti, an Argentine, set up Prensa Latina. Most members of the Rebel Army were peasants, but I'd been a student at the preuniversity level. Masetti knew this and tried to recruit me. "How would you like to be a journalist and help found a Latin American press agency?" he asked.

I went to talk to Che.

"Che, Masetti is proposing I go work with him in Prensa Latina."

"I'll tell you this for the second time: Don't be a jerk. We need you in the army. Tell Masetti to go look for journalists somewhere else. You can't go."

That was another lesson.

The third time I got this type of lesson from Che was after he'd been named head of the National Bank. One of my sisters called and said her mother-in-law was dying in Macao, and she needed fifty dollars for a visa. She asked me to talk to Che.

So naively, I did.

"Che, my sister, whose mother-in-law is dying in Macao, needs fifty dollars to pay for a visa to go visit her."

Che stuck his hand in his pocket.

"All I have is 125 pesos." At the time, all officers got a wage of 125 pesos a month.

"If you need it, take it," he said. "But I don't have any dollars."

What a lesson! I've never forgotten it.

In my life as a revolutionary I've had a number of privileges. Most importantly for my revolutionary education, I served under three great leaders. First, Fidel in the Sierra Maestra. Second, as a combatant in Che's column. Third, beginning in 1965 I worked for nearly seven years directly with Raúl Castro, as aide to the minister of the Revolutionary Armed Forces. During this time I also had the privilege of working under Juan Almeida, who for a year and a half filled in as minister while Raúl was studying at the Military Academy.

That for me has been a great privilege. To have worked under leaders of that stature, to have known them, to have been under their command, and to have learned from them.

Chinese in Cuba

WATERS: The three of you had quite different experiences growing up as Cubans of Chinese origin. Tell us a little about the Chinese emigration to Cuba. What place did it have in Cuba's history?

SÍO WONG: The story begins in 1840, with the start of the first Opium War in China. Using opium imports as their main lever, the European colonial powers set out to dominate China. They had already introduced opium into the country in large amounts. Realizing the impact the growing opium trade was having on Chinese society and the Chinese people, the Manchu emperor issued a decree prohibiting its entry. The emperor sent a representative to Canton. A big operation was organized, destroying tens of thousands of chests of opium. The colonial powers, with England in the lead, used this as the pretext to go to war against China.

The Opium War ended in 1842, with China's defeat. Afterward, the colonial powers forced the Chinese rulers to make a number of concessions. First, China ceded Hong Kong to England and opened five ports to commerce—the ports of Canton (today Guangzhou), Amoy (today Xiamen), Fuzhou, Ningbo, and Shanghai. Over the next two decades China was forced to make more concessions, not just to the English but to other colonial powers too—the Americans, the French, the

Ports of origin of Chinese indentured laborers arriving in Cuba

RUSSIA

MONGOLIA

Ürümqi

BEIJING

C H I N A

KOREA

Xi'an

Shanghai

Lhasa

NEPAL

BHUTAN

BANGLADESH

INDIA

Fuzhou

Guangzhou (Canton)

VIETNAM

MYANMAR

0   500   1000 miles

JIANGXI

FUJIAN

Fuzhou

Xiamen (Amoy)

Taiwan

GUANGXI

GUANGDONG

Shantou (Swatow)

Guangzhou (Canton)

Huangpu (Whampoa)

Aomen (Macao)

Xianggang (Hong Kong)

● Cities
------- Province borders
⚓ Ports of origin

0   50   100   150 miles

Hainan

Based on map prepared by Fundación Fernando Ortiz

Portuguese, and so on. China opened different ports to them, from which they carried on their operations.

The English realized they could profit from dominating China in another way. They started to contract Chinese labor for exploitation in their colonies here in the Western Hemisphere: Trinidad and Tobago, Jamaica, Guyana, Barbados.

The Spanish Crown saw that this could be an alternative to African slaves, to develop the sugar industry here in Cuba above all.

Twenty-five years earlier, in 1817, England and Spain had signed a treaty abolishing the African slave trade. Spain didn't comply, of course, and continued bringing in slaves from Africa in violation of the treaty. In fact, more slaves were brought in than ever before. But since they couldn't do it as openly, they weren't able to bring in the amount of labor they needed.[15]

Another factor also influenced Spain's decision to bring in Chinese indentured labor. The 1841 census conducted by the Spanish indicated there were 1,017,000 people in Cuba, of whom only 418,000 were classified as white. There were 150,000 people in the category of free mestizos, and 432,000 slaves. That is, there were substantially more slaves and free men and women of mixed blood than there were whites.

There had already been a number of slave revolts. In 1844 there was a very famous case, the "Ladder Conspiracy," in which Plácido, a brilliant poet of mixed blood, was executed by firing squad. Some historians have said they don't know whether there really was such a conspiracy, or whether it was just a pretext by the Spanish authorities for repressive measures to try to forestall rebellions. But slave revolts were something they were very concerned about. The victorious

15. See glossary, Slavery in Cuba.

slave rebellion in Haiti was an ever-present reminder.[16]

Taking their cue from the English, in 1844 the Spanish established a company in the port of Amoy to traffic in Chinese labor. They set up a barracks there. Amoy, or Xiamen, is right across from Taiwan, on the Straits of Taiwan.

The Chinese were contracted for a period of eight years. Pay was four pesos a month, plus food and clothing. They had to work for whoever bought or rebought their contract, which sold for seventy pesos. Thus they were indentured laborers. They were promised that after eight years they could choose to return to China or stay in the country as a free laborer. But they had no choice, of course. They had to stay since they didn't have money for the return passage.

The first shipment of contract laborers arrived in Cuba on June 3, 1847, aboard the Spanish ship *Oquendo*. Two hundred six arrived on that first ship. They disembarked at the port of Regla on Havana Bay, the same port the Spanish used for bringing in African slaves. They were put in barracks, and their contracts were sold to wealthy landowners, who treated them the same as slaves. On June 12 an English merchant ship, the *Duke of Argyle,* arrived with another 365 Chinese. A number had died during the journey, which took between four and five months. So in 1847 these nearly 600 were the first indentured Chinese to arrive.

Subsequently, partly in response to publicity about the mistreatment they had suffered, contracting was suspended by the Spanish Crown. But the queen authorized its resumption in 1852.

It's estimated that between 1848 and 1874, 141,000 Chinese were shipped out to Cuba, with 10–15 percent dying in passage. That's roughly the same number that went to the United

16. See glossary, Haitian Revolution.

States during those years. In proportion to population, however, emigration to Cuba was far more significant. In 1870 Cuba's population was 1.4 million; the population of the US was 38 million—more than 25 times larger.

These indentured laborers were put to work on sugar plantations and other agricultural estates. Conditions were very difficult. First of all, they didn't know the language. Second, they didn't know how to use a machete, how to cut cane. They didn't know how other tools were handled.

A large number of Chinese escaped to the hills, just as African slaves did. There were places known as *palenques*, where runaway black slaves—*cimarrones*—went, and some Chinese did the same. Others committed suicide. They preferred suicide to continued mistreatment, to being treated as slaves.

In addition to direct emigration from China, between 1865 and 1875 some 5,000 Chinese made their way to Cuba from the United States. Many had built the railroads there. Recently I saw the movie *Wyatt Earp*, starring Kevin Costner. In it you see Chinese building the railroads across the United States. Well, many of these Chinese subsequently emigrated to Cuba, trying to escape the conditions they faced in the United States.

War of Independence

On October 10, 1868, Cuba's War of Independence began.[17] Slaves were freed by the independence forces, and the contracts of all Chinese indentured laborers were declared null and void by the Republic in Arms.[18] Thousands of Africans and Chinese joined the struggle. There were battalions and companies composed entirely of Chinese.

17. See glossary, Cuban independence wars.

18. See glossary, Republic in Arms.

On the corner of Línea and L streets in Havana, there's a monument to the Chinese who fought in the war of independence. On it is a plaque with a statement by General Gonzalo de Quesada, who was secretary of José Martí's Cuban Revolutionary Party. "There was not a single Chinese Cuban deserter," Gonzalo de Quesada says. "There was not a single Chinese Cuban traitor." Not a single case is known of any Chinese who helped the Spanish. Not one. Keep in mind that many native-born Cubans were part of the Volunteers, a notoriously brutal corps of Cubans who covered police duties so Spanish troops could fight the independence forces.

A number of years ago Fidel asked me if it's known how many Chinese participated in the 1868–98 independence wars. It hasn't been possible to determine, I said, since the Chinese used to change their names. They'd put down "Gustavo González" or "Ramón Fernández." They'd often take their masters' surname. Chinese names don't appear on the army rolls. Some historians estimate the number of Chinese combatants at 6,000. But no one knows for sure. It's possible there were more.

Then Fidel asked how many participated in the final war of liberation, that of 1957–59. How many sons of Chinese took part?

I told him we didn't know that either. Because unless the person's surname comes from the father, the next generation loses it. So there are many people whose Chinese ancestry can't be determined simply from looking at their names. Take, for instance, Esteban Lazo Hernández. Today he is the head of political education and orientation for the party's Political Bureau; his grandfather was Chinese. Bárbara Castillo Cuestas, minister of domestic trade; her grandmother was Chinese. Lázaro Barredo, vice president of the International Relations Commission of the National Assembly; he too had

Chinese grandparents. These Cuban leaders are all examples of people of Chinese ancestry. But they've lost their Chinese surnames.

CHOY: To give you an idea of the scope of Chinese participation in the war, in the battle of Las Guásimas alone, in 1874, there was a battalion of 500 native-born Chinese who fought under the command of General Máximo Gómez. An entire battalion.

SÍO WONG: In addition to being combatants, Chinese helped in other ways, such as contributing food.

My father, for example, had a little store in Matanzas during the 1895–98 war. One day he was upbraided by the colonial authorities for giving out some items from his store free of charge to a group of *mambises* who were passing by.[19]

"Why didn't you charge them?" he was asked.

"Well, the Spaniards pass by too and take things," was the excuse he gave. "And they don't pay either."

That's an example.

Many Chinese in the cities also contributed by providing information. To the Spanish colonial authorities, all Chinese looked the same. So Chinese would pass undetected when they went to the towns and cities to find out information about the Spanish troops. If anyone questioned them, they'd just say, "I no understand, I no understand."

WATERS: Did most of the Chinese in Cuba still speak mainly Chinese at that time? Or had they begun to speak Spanish? Or both?

SÍO WONG: The Chinese came here not knowing Spanish. Later they began learning a few words, but during the war communication was very difficult. That's why they were organized in separate companies or battalions.

19. See glossary, *Mambises.*

There's an anecdote about an officer named Colonel Hernández serving under General Ignacio Agramonte. Hernández commanded a Chinese battalion, and he'd had it up to here with them. Since the officer and the troops often didn't understand each other, there were acts of indiscipline. So the colonel asked to meet with Agramonte. As the colonel approached the tent, Agramonte already knew why he was coming.

"Colonel, you must be so proud of your battalion," the general said as soon as they got inside. "You must be so proud of that heroic battalion, and how they love you as their commander." Think of it! General Ignacio Agramonte starts lauding the Chinese, how they loved their commander, their heroic attitude in this battle and that battle, how good they were. The colonel undoubtedly didn't say a word about what he'd really come to talk about, which was to ask to be transferred, since he was tired of dealing with the Chinese troops.

There's a fact that also illustrates the extent of Chinese participation in our wars of independence.

In 1901, after the final independence war was over, a constitution was approved. It included a provision—Article 65—that any foreigner who had fought for ten years for Cuba's freedom, arms in hand, would be considered Cuban by birth. He could even be president of the republic. That provision was included because of Máximo Gómez, who had commanded the army and was Dominican. But Máximo Gómez didn't accept the proposal. He said no, he was Dominican, a foreigner. A foreigner! Imagine!

Only four individuals qualified under that special constitutional provision: General Máximo Gómez, who was Dominican; General Carlos Roloff, who was Polish; and two Chinese—Lieutenant Colonel José Bu and Captain José Tolón (Lai Wa). They had fought in the three wars. Some historians suggest

Chinese fighters in Cuba's 1868–78 independence war.

José Martí National Library

that Rius Rivera, who was Puerto Rican, also qualified, but that remains a disputed question. Anyway, these examples speak to the participation of Chinese in the independence wars.

KOPPEL: When did the system of contract labor end?

sío WONG: "Good treatment" for Chinese, "as religion and humanity demand," was recommended in a Royal Order by Queen Isabel II in 1847. The order also suggested that Chinese and blacks be kept apart.

In 1857 the Royal Council put a cap on the number of Chinese allowed to enter Cuba. And in 1860, owing to pressures from other foreign powers in China, Spain had to agree to prohibit sending Chinese contract labor to the American continent. Despite this, Chinese contract laborers in fact continued to be brought in until 1874.

During Cuba's independence war, the Spanish crown became alarmed at the Chinese role in the independence army. So in 1871 the crown issued another Royal Decree. It stated that based on "the difficulties" and "grave damage" caused by immigrants breaking "their commitments," Chinese laborers were endangering "public order" and aiding "the enemies of the nation." Therefore, "in the interests of tranquility," the bringing of Chinese contract laborers into Cuba was suspended.

On November 17, 1877, the Peking Agreement was signed by China and Spain, ending the criminal trade of indentured Chinese labor in Cuba. But Cuba itself was not informed about this until June 29, 1879, when it was published in the *Gaceta de La Habana*.

Creation of Chinese community

HAWKINS: How did Chinatown in Havana—and elsewhere in Cuba—develop?

sío WONG: As Chinese completed their eight-year contracts and were set free, most stayed alive by becoming street vendors. They sold fruit, fried foods, vegetables, and other things. These vendors established the first Chinatowns. There were a few small restaurants and stands on the corner of Zanja and Rayo streets in Havana. A Chinese district gradually grew up around there, where people spoke both Chinese and Spanish. Several Chinese-language newspapers were established. In 1867 members of the Chinese community formed the first Chinese society, the Kit Yi Tong.

Eventually the Chinese district in Havana came to be the most important Chinatown in Latin America. Surpassed in the Americas only by San Francisco.

WATERS: What was the geographic spread of the Chinese population?

SÍO WONG: Initially the Chinese were concentrated in the provinces where the sugar industry was most highly developed, such as Havana, Matanzas, Villa Clara, and Oriente. But later on they spread to all the provinces and cities.[20]

Most Chinese became merchants and traders. Food services, laundries, services of that type. If you didn't make it in Las Tunas, you went to Camagüey, or someplace else. Like Chui's father did. Through this process the Chinese spread throughout the country.

WATERS: Virtually all the Chinese who came as indentured laborers were men—I've read that in some years it was over 99 percent. That must have had a big impact on the development of the Chinese community.

SÍO WONG: That's clearly one reason there was a lot of intermarriage. Many Chinese men married Cuban women. Among the Chinese there weren't the same pressures against intermarriage you see in some other communities—the Jewish community, for example.

20. See map showing spread of Chinese population in Cuba on p. 29.

Chinatown in Havana, late 19th century.

There's an interesting case in my own family. We were fourteen brothers and sisters—six girls and eight boys. My mother insisted that all the girls had to marry men both of whose parents were Chinese. None of them could marry the son of a Chinese and a Cuban; he had to be the son of a Chinese man and a Chinese woman. So that's what happened. And all us boys married Cuban women.

WATERS: What was the scope of the Chinese emigration to Cuba after 1874, when the system of contract labor was effectively ended?

SÍO WONG: It decreased. But because of the prevailing conditions in China—a backward, semicolonial country in which landlords, warlords, and foreign imperialists criminally exploited millions of peasants and workers—many Chinese, in desperation, emigrated to a number of countries, including Cuba, in search of better conditions of life.

Discrimination against Chinese

WATERS: What types of discrimination and racism did the Chinese face?

CHUI: There were many things. For example, I remember the taunt, "Chino Manila pa' Canton." People would see us and they'd shout that. In effect, "Chinaman from Manila, go back to Canton!" You remember that, don't you, Sío?

SÍO WONG: Oh yes.

CHUI: That's how we were viewed by some people.

KOPPEL: Why did they shout "Chino Manila"? What was that about?

SÍO WONG: Some contract laborers arrived by way of the Philippines, which was then a Spanish colony too. "Chinaman from Manila" was a derogatory expression for all Chinese.

CHUI: I also remember how they used to yell, "Narra, hey narra!"

SÍO WONG: Calling a Chinese person in Cuba "narra" is like saying "nigger" to a black person in the United States. In Cuba the comparable slur for blacks was "niche." Blacks were called "niche" and Chinese were called "narra." "Hey, narra!" It was an offensive, insulting word, like "slant-eye" or "chink." There was discrimination against blacks. And there was discrimination against Chinese. There were places neither could go. The racial discrimination took economic forms too.

WATERS: For example?

SÍO WONG: Access to education, for instance. There were private schools and private universities they couldn't attend. And there were private clinics they were barred from, where health care was better than what was available to the poor.

CHUI: There were elite clubs, too. Take the case of the owner of the Rosita Hotel, for example. He was a millionaire but he was mulatto—and they wouldn't let him into one of the major clubs. This same man, under Batista, built a social club—Club Alfonso—for mulattos and blacks, but later they wouldn't let blacks in. Only mulattos, provided they didn't look too mulatto!

SÍO WONG: There were elite places where you didn't see blacks. And Chinese couldn't go either. There were beaches like Tarará outside Havana, for example, where Chinese and blacks—or any poor person—couldn't go. Or Brisas del Mar, east of Havana. This was a private beach, and they wouldn't let you in.

In the Miramar section of Havana, there was a special private police force paid for by the rich. At night they'd patrol the streets, demanding, "Where's your identification? What are you doing around here?"

Blacks were the main target of that kind of discrimination. In Santa Clara, for example, there was a promenade in the park for whites and a different promenade for blacks. Chinese were allowed to use the promenade for whites. But the Chinese were discriminated against in many ways too. Choy told how they wouldn't let his friend into a dance with his girlfriend because it was for whites only.

So there was discrimination against blacks and Chinese. There was also discrimination because of sex. There was discrimination against the poor.

Class divisions in Chinese community

WATERS: What was the class structure of the Chinese population?

SÍO WONG: They were shopkeepers primarily. But the Chinese community was far from homogeneous. It was divided between rich and poor. There were very rich merchants and businessmen who were quite powerful economically. There was a Chinese-owned bank. There was a Chinese Chamber of Commerce. There were Chinese millionaires.

There was one millionaire who built a house by the Almendares River here in Havana that is now the Pavo Real Restaurant. It's said that it's an exact replica of a house near Hong Kong, on the banks of the Pearl River, which belonged to the man's father. He sent for the architects, they duplicated it exactly. That house is still there.

Then there were the poorest Chinese, the street vendors, and so forth.

One can talk of discrimination—we Chinese were discriminated against racially because we were Chinese. But I would say that the economic discrimination by the rich against the poor was greater.

WATERS: Over the first sixty years of the twentieth century, after what's known in the United States as the Spanish-American War, Washington was the dominant imperialist power in Cuba. How did that affect the Chinese community?

síO WONG: The US government had a great deal of influence on the Cuban government during those decades. We were a nominally independent republic, with a capitalist system. The US ambassador dictated policy. Sumner Welles, Franklin D. Roosevelt's ambassador in the 1930s, was infamous for imposing Washington's interests, for example. The US military mission had great influence on the Cuban army.

Washington's domination was reflected in the weight the US-backed Chiang Kai-shek dictatorship had in the Chinese community here. Chiang Kai-shek led the counterrevolutionary forces that fled to Taiwan after they were overthrown by the Chinese Revolution of 1949. His party, the Kuomintang, or Nationalist Party, was led in Cuba by a group of wealthy merchants and had considerable influence among the Chinese population. Before 1959, for example, the Chung Wah Casino[21]—an umbrella group of all the Chinese societies— was under the influence of the Kuomintang.

After 1949 the Cuban government had diplomatic relations with Taiwan, not Beijing, and that Chinese consulate played a role in the Chinese community. Its office was next to the office of the president of the Chung Wah Casino in Havana.

As I said, the Chinese population here was divided between rich and poor. Among the rich, the impact of US domination and influence was not much different from what it was for the Cuban oligarchy as a whole.

With the triumph of the revolution in 1959 there was a polarization in the Chinese community similar to the rest of society. The wealthy Chinese merchants and businessmen, as well as some of the smaller Chinese merchants, abandoned the country. The majority of the Chinese, however, joined the revolution. The Kuomintang Society, which had been affili-

21. The word *casino* in Spanish in this case means society or club.

ated to the Kuomintang Party in Taiwan, ceased to exist. Its offices, and the leadership of the Chung Wah Casino, were taken over by revolutionaries. In September 1960 Cuba cut its ties with Taiwan and formally recognized the People's Republic of China, the first country in Latin America to do so.

WATERS: Where did the Chinese who left Cuba go?

SÍO WONG: Some to Taiwan. Many to the United States, Canada, Central America, and to other countries.

WATERS: In New York there are still many Chinese Cuban restaurants, which were established soon after 1959.

SÍO WONG: There's a funny story about that. In 1988 the agreement ending the war in Angola and granting independence to Namibia was signed at the United Nations in New York City.[22] A group of Cuban generals who had participated in the defense of Angola against the South African invasion went to New York for the signing.[23]

One day some of them wanted to eat Chinese food, and a compañero from the Cuban Mission to the United Nations took them to a restaurant in Chinatown. When they got there, a number of compañeros, using their poor English, tried to order food. But they were having great difficulty.

After a while the guy in the restaurant stopped them and said in fluent Spanish, "Save your effort, fellas, I'm Cuban."

After 1959

HAWKINS: What's the most important measure taken after 1959 to combat discrimination against Chinese and blacks?

SÍO WONG: The principal measure was the revolution itself.

22. See part II.

23. The six Cuban generals in New York for the signing were Abelardo Colomé, Leopoldo Cintra Frías, Ramón Espinosa, Víctor Schueg, Rafael Moracén, and Pascual Martínez Gil.

It was no single action, although a number of measures were very important. Like banning discrimination in hiring. And turning all beaches into public property, open to everybody.[24] But the socialist revolution was made precisely to eliminate inequalities. To bring about social justice. To end discrimination against blacks, women, and the poor. To close the gulf between rich and poor.

KOPPEL: I've heard that a Chinese Cuban militia unit helped carry out the nationalizations of the big capitalist holdings in 1960 and was instrumental during the early years of the revolution in eliminating drugs, prostitution, and gambling from Havana's Chinatown. Is that true?

SÍO WONG: That was the José Wong Brigade, which was part of the Revolutionary National Militia. It was formed in early 1960. José Wong was a young revolutionary who came to Cuba from Canton in the early 1920s for economic reasons. He became a revolutionary fighter against the Machado dictatorship here in Cuba, along with Julio Antonio Mella and Rafael Trejo, and joined the Communist Party. In 1930 he was taken prisoner and assassinated in Havana's Príncipe prison.

Militia units were formed by the Cuban people everywhere during the revolution's first days. There were student militias at the university, worker militias in the factories, peasant militias in the countryside. In my neighborhood of San Lázaro, for example, we created a militia named after Pepe Valladares, a martyr from there killed in the struggle against Batista. By

24. On March 22, 1959, in what became known as the "Proclamation against Racism," Prime Minister Fidel Castro presented the initial measures being taken by the revolutionary government to ban racial discrimination in Cuba. A translation of the speech was published in the *Militant*, April 19, 1999, and is available online at themilitant.com.

Courtesy Moisés Sío Wong

In response to increasing US military threats, Cuban working people organized into popular militias to defend revolution.

Top: Members of Militia of the Retail Commerce Workers Union, 1959. On right is Pedro Eng, second in command of militia unit.

Bottom right: November 1960 letter from then-captain Rogelio Acevedo, director of National Revolutionary Militias, authorizing Eng to organize the José Wong Brigade, composed of militia members of Chinese descent. It played an important role in breaking hold of Chinese Cuban capitalists over Havana's Chinatown and eradicating the infamous drug, prostitution, and gambling businesses they controlled.

Bottom left: José Wong, whose name the brigade took, was a Chinese-born Cuban revolutionary assassinated in 1930s by the Machado dictatorship.

late 1959, with the number of new militia units still increasing, they began to unify into a single body, the Revolutionary National Militia.

The José Wong Brigade, which did the things you mentioned, also participated in defeating the mercenary invasion at Playa Girón in 1961.[25]

KOPPEL: What's the situation of the Chinese community in Cuba today?

SÍO WONG: There are now only about 300 Chinese in Cuba who were born in China. There has been no significant immigration since the revolution in 1959, so the remaining Cubans born in China are all elderly.

Chinese societies like the Chung Wah Casino have worked to rescue the cultural traditions of the Chinese community. But it's been difficult, since nearly all the children of Chinese are fully integrated into Cuban society. We've tried to bring them together, but undoubtedly it's not the same as in other countries. The historic Chinese associations that exist have forty or fifty members, and they've now opened up to third-, fourth-, fifth-, even sixth-generation Chinese to make the societies a little bigger. But they survive. You can see their buildings in Havana's Chinatown.

WATERS: One of the projects of the Cuba-China Friendship Association, which you're the president of, is the restoration of Havana's Chinatown. Is that something recent?

SÍO WONG: In 1993 a group of Chinese descendants approached the Cuba-China Friendship Association, soliciting its support for a restoration project for Chinatown. Out of this came the Chinatown Promotional Group. The project has two main aims. One is preserving the traditions, art, and culture of Chinese in Cuba. The other is to revitalize Havana's

25. See glossary, Playa Girón.

Chinatown economically and commercially.

From the cultural point of view, we've registered significant advances. The Chinese House of Arts and Traditions holds exhibits and literary competitions, as well as contests in the visual arts, dance, music, theater. It even offers instruction in the Chinese language.

The project to rescue Chinatown has received support from various Chinese societies across the island, including the Chung Wah Casino, the principal center of the Chinese community here.

The embassy of the People's Republic of China has given its support, too. For example, the archway at the entrance to Chinatown was donated by Chinese deputy prime minister Li Langqing.

Currently the Promotional Group functions under the office of the official historian of the City of Havana, compañero Eusebio Leal. That's the office responsible for the enormous project to restore Old Havana, and they're in the best position to move this ambitious project forward too. But the Cuba-China Friendship Association will continue giving all its support.

Cuba's example

WATERS: There are Chinese minorities in other countries of Latin America, as well as the United States. But the conditions they live and work under are very different from those in Cuba today. How do you see the changes that have taken place in your lifetime?

SÍO WONG: In 1999 there was an international conference on the Chinese diaspora held in Cuba. It was initiated by the International Society for the Study of Chinese Overseas (ISSCO). The organization's president, Wang Gungwu, who lives in Singapore, and a professor from California, Ling-chi Wang, initiated the event here. It was sponsored by the University of Havana, and representatives of Chinese communities in various countries participated. Many came from the United States, from Canada, from Southeast Asia.

I recall that the president and his wife asked me, "How is it possible that you, a descendant of Chinese, occupy a high government post, are a deputy in the National Assembly, and a general of the Armed Forces? How is that possible?"

The answer doesn't lie in the degree of Chinese participation in the war of independence. That is worth studying, since nothing similar happened in any other country where Chinese indentured workers were taken. But here too, before the triumph of the revolution, we Chinese were discriminated against.

What's the difference in the experience of Chinese in Cuba and other countries of the diaspora? The difference is that here a socialist revolution took place. The revolution uprooted discrimination based on the color of a person's skin. That's because, above all, we overturned the property relations that create not only economic but also social inequality between rich and poor.

That's what made it possible for the son of Chinese immigrants to become a government representative, or anything else. Here discrimination—against blacks, against Chinese, against women, against the poor—was ended. Cubans of Chinese descent are integrated.

To historians and others who want to study the question, I say that you have to understand that the Chinese community here in Cuba is different from Peru, Brazil, Argentina, or Canada.

And that difference is the triumph of a socialist revolution.

"The Spanish crown brought indentured Chinese labor as an alternative to African slaves. Between 1848 and 1874, some 141,000 left China for Cuba and a similar number went to the US. In 1870 Cuba's population was 1.4 million; in the US it was 38 million."

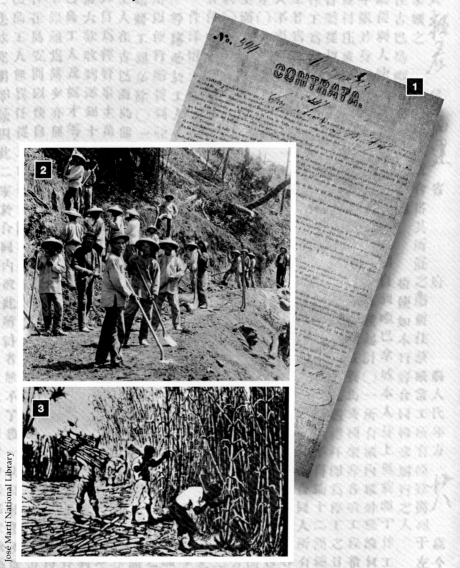

José Martí National Library

1. Contract for Chinese indentured laborers, printed in Chinese (background) and Spanish, 1861.

2. Chinese workers building railroad in United States, mid-19th century. Thousands later emigrated from the US to Cuba.

3. Slaves cutting sugarcane in Cuba.

2

1

1. Soldiers in Cuba's independence army, 1898.

2. Chinese Cuban independence fighters. Many Chinese soldiers in Cuba's first independence war were escaped indentured workers.

3. Monument in Havana to Chinese who fought in independence wars. On its base are the words of General Gonzalo de Quesada: "There was not a single Chinese Cuban deserter. There was not a single Chinese Cuban traitor."

"Thousands of Chinese participated in Cuba's wars of independence. Of these, it is said, there was not a single deserter nor a single traitor."

4. Ramón Estrada, who fought in 1895–98 independence war. His father was Chinese, his mother Cuban.

5. Captain José Tolón (Lai Wa), one of four combatants born outside Cuba who through their military record in all three independence wars earned the right to serve as president of new republic.

"Before the revolution there was discrimination against blacks and Chinese. Moreover, the Chinese population was itself class-divided. There were both rich and poor."

After bonded labor came to an end, in the late 19th century, Chinese communities developed across Cuba. Most Chinese were engaged in petty commerce and trade. Some became very wealthy.

1. Reception for Chinese government minister, held in Chinese Chamber of Commerce, Havana, 1940s. Painting in background is of Chiang Kai-shek, Franklin Roosevelt, Winston Churchill, and Madame Chiang Kai-shek in Cairo, 1943.

2. Chinese vendor in Havana, late 1940s or early 1950s.

3. Gustavo Chui's father, José Chui (left), and uncle Rafael Wong.
4. Chui (inset), age 6, 1944.
5. Armando Choy, age 12, with father Armando, 1946.
6. Moisés Sío Wong, fourth from left, age 6, with sisters Orquídea and Sofía, brother Julio, mother Julia, and father, Santiago, 1944.

"The Chinese district in Havana came to be the most important Chinatown in Latin America, surpassed in the Americas only by San Francisco."

Photos: Bohemia

1. Laundry in Havana, late 1940s. "As Chinese left the sugar plantations," Sío Wong explained, "they spread to all the provinces and cities. Most became petty merchants and traders—restaurants, laundries, services of that type."

2. During the 1940s and 1950s there were four Chinese-language dailies in Cuba. In photo, restaurant patrons reading *Man Sen Yat Po,* newspaper of Kuomintang Party in Cuba, 1949.

3. Store in Havana's Chinatown, 1952.
4. Chinese vegetable shop, Havana, 1949.
5. Traditional street festival in Havana, 1940s.

Bohemia

Photos: Granma

"We were becoming increasingly conscious of the unjust character of the Batista regime. When the July 26 Movement was founded, we joined."

Bohemia

Granma

1. On March 10, 1952, Fulgencio Batista established a brutal dictatorship backed by Washington. In photo, Batista with troops on day of coup.

2. Fidel Castro organized a revolutionary movement to overthrow the tyranny. It assaulted the Moncada garrison in Santiago de Cuba on July 26, 1953. In photo, Castro and other captured combatants being led to jail a week later.

3. Armando Choy (front row, left) in student protest against Batista dictatorship, Santa Clara, May 20, 1957. The demonstration was quickly broken up by police. Choy and others were arrested later that day.

4. Student demonstration in Havana under attack by cops, November 1956.

5. Gerardo Abreu (Fontán) and **6.** Ñico López, leaders of July 26 Movement Youth Brigades, helped recruit Sío Wong to revolutionary movement.

"'Hey Fidel, even the Chinese are here!' That was how I was greeted when I got to the Sierra Maestra."

—MOISÉS SÍO WONG

Courtesy Moisés Sío Wong

Courtesy Gustavo Chui

Courtesy Armando Choy

Photos: Granma

During the 1956–58 revolutionary war, thousands of young workers, peasants, and students joined the Rebel Army and July 26 Movement to fight the Batista dictatorship.

1. Moisés Sío Wong after battle of Placetas, December 24, 1958.

2. Gustavo Chui, left, with members of Rebel Army tank company outside Havana, shortly after revolution's victory.

3. Armando Choy (back row, second from right), with fellow Rebel Army combatants, near Fomento, late 1958.

4. Sergio González (El Curita), at right, a leader of July 26 Movement underground in Havana. Photo shows him at printshop where clandestine revolutionary newspaper was produced. In February 1958 Fidel Castro sent Sío Wong on mission to Havana to instruct González to leave for the Sierra. González insisted on staying and days later was killed by Batista's police.

5. Fidel Castro and victorious Rebel Army columns entering Santiago de Cuba, January 1, 1959. That night, Gustavo Chui was among those guarding the rally where Castro addressed tens of thousands.

"What was the most important measure taken to uproot discrimination against Chinese and blacks in Cuba? It was the socialist revolution itself."

Gilberto Ante

Henry Wallace

1959 agrarian reform and 1961 literacy drive, as well as March 1959 decree banning discrimination based on race, were sweeping measures that defined the working-class trajectory of the revolution.

1. Fidel Castro and María de la Cruz Sentmanat, 106-year-old former slave who learned to read and write during literacy drive.

2. Beach in Havana that was formerly a "whites-only" private preserve. One of revolution's first measures was to open every public space to all.

Granma

3. Members of Chinese New Democracy Alliance, an organization of revolutionary Chinese Cubans, at rally in support of nationalization of US capitalist holdings, July 10, 1960.

4. Mass meeting in Havana's Chinatown, October 2, 1960, in honor of 11th anniversary of Chinese Revolution.

"We put all of Cuba behind the Angola effort. We felt it was something vital."

Granma

Courtesy Armando Choy

Courtesy Moisés Sío Wong

Photos: Courtesy Gustavo Chui

In November 1975, the government of Angola asked Cuba for help in defeating a South African invasion. Some 375,000 Cuban volunteer combatants took part in that 16-year mission, alongside fighters from Angola and Namibia. They dealt a crushing defeat to the South African army at Cuito Cuanavale in 1988.

1. Raúl Díaz Argüelles, first head of Cuba's military mission in Angola, killed by land mine in opening weeks of campaign. One-quarter of Cuban volunteers who died in Angola were officers.

2. Armando Choy (center) in Angola, March 1981. Next to him are a Namibian combatant (second from right) and General Ramón Pardo Guerra (far right).

3. Moisés Sío Wong (second from left) leading operation in Angola, 1976.

4. Gustavo Chui (at front) reviewing Cuban tank brigade in Luanda, 1987.

5. Chui's jeep, destroyed by antitank mine, March 1988. Chui was critically wounded, losing a leg.

"We were not fighting just for Angola. Breaking the back of the apartheid army at Cuito Cuanavale hastened the destruction of the apartheid system itself."

Granma

Margrethe Siem/Militant

1. Following defeat at Cuito Cuanavale, South African government sued for peace. In photo, signing of accords at United Nations, December 1988. Left to right: South African defense minister Magnus Malan and foreign minister Pik Botha; UN secretary-general Javier Pérez de Cuéllar; US secretary of state George Shultz; Angolan foreign minister Afonso Van-Dúnem and ambassador to US António dos Santos França; Cuban foreign minister Isidoro Malmierca and Gen. Abelardo Colomé.

2. On February 11, 1990, less than two years after signing of accords, Nelson Mandela walked free after 27 years in prison. Namibia declared its independence a month later. Here, Johannesburg, South Africa, rally greets Mandela, March 17, 1990.

Jon Hillson/Militant

Mary-Alice Waters/Militant

3. Ours was "a mass revolutionary army of the people," both men and women, said army general Raúl Castro. Here, combatants of women's antiaircraft unit return to Havana, May 1989.

4. Mandela and Castro in Matanzas, Cuba, July 26, 1991. "We in Africa are used to being victims of countries wanting to carve up our territory or subvert our sovereignty," Mandela told the world. "It is unparalleled in African history to have another people rise to our defense."

"Some day we may have to erect a monument to the Special Period." —FIDEL CASTRO

With the fall of the regimes in the Soviet Union and Eastern Europe in 1989–91, Cuba lost 85 percent of its foreign trade. A devastating economic crisis known in Cuba as the Special Period ensued. Millions of workers, farmers, and youth organized to confront the challenges. By 1996 the worst of the economic decline had been halted.

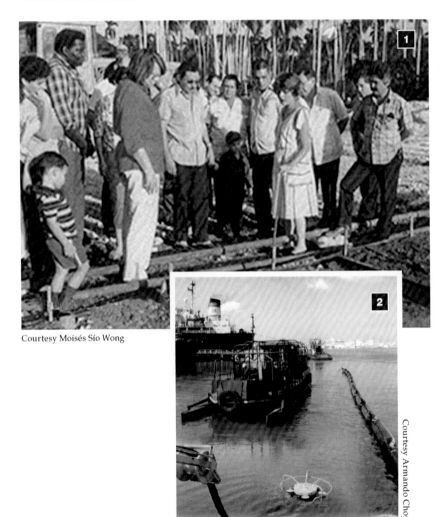

Courtesy Moisés Sío Wong

Courtesy Armando Choy

1. In 1991 a program was launched to turn vacant lots into vegetable gardens. In photo, Raúl Castro (center) at experimental *organopónico* in Havana, December 27, 1987. To right, in dress is Ana Luisa Pérez, engineer who pioneered this form of production. In plaid shirt, Esteban Lazo; front left, Vilma Espín.

2. Despite Cuba's severe shortages, longstanding challenges like the contamination of Havana Bay were taken on during the Special Period.

Jonathan Silberman/Militant

Angel González Baldrich/Granma

Some economic measures during Special Period led to greater inequality, undermining social solidarity. Spearheaded by the Union of Young Communists (UJC), the Battle of Ideas was launched in 1999 to organize new educational and cultural opportunities for youth across Cuba.

3. Preuniversity class for workers at Camilo Cienfuegos sugar mill in Havana province, January 2003. Tens of thousands of workers and youth receive a regular wage as they study.

4. The UJC mobilized youth to help renovate and build schools throughout the country, making it possible to reduce class size and improve the quality of educational programs.

"We defend ourselves with our own forces and means, based on each Cuban having a weapon—a rifle, a mine, a rock. It's the war of the entire people."

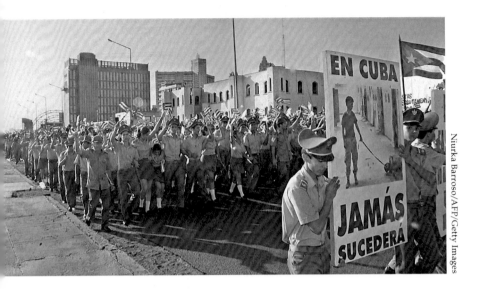

Niurka Barroso/AFP/Getty Images

March in Havana in front of US Interests Section, March 2004. Sign shows infamous photo of degrading US treatment of prisoners in Abu Ghraib prison in Iraq. "In Cuba this will *never* happen," it reads.

PART II

Strengthening the revolution

Cuban and Angolan combatants celebrating capture of South African tank during battle of Cuito Cuanavale, Angola, 1988.

Cuba's internationalist mission to Angola, 1975–91

Between November 1975 and May 1991, some 425,000 Cuban volunteers served in Angola in response to requests by the Angolan government. They helped defend that newly independent country against a decade and a half of military aggression, including two major invasions by the white-supremacist regime of South Africa and its African allies, backed by Washington. The volunteers included 375,000 combatants as well as 50,000 doctors, teachers, and other civilian workers.

The internationalist effort was named Operation Carlota, after the Cuban heroine Carlota, an African-born woman enslaved in Cuba who in 1843 led a rebellion in the sugar-producing province of Matanzas, Cuba.

South Africa's first invasion began in October 1975, when its troops crossed Angola's southern border. At the same time, forces of the US-backed Mobutu dictatorship in Zaire and the National Front for the Liberation of Angola (FNLA) moved down from the north.[1] Their goal was to capture the capital city of Luanda before November 11, when the country was to become independent from Portuguese rule, and block the installation of a government led by the Popular Movement for the Liberation of Angola (MPLA).

1. The Democratic Republic of the Congo was called Zaire from 1971 to 1997. See glossary for FNLA, MPLA, and UNITA.

At the MPLA leadership's urgent request for help, thousands of Cuban internationalist combatants were rapidly mobilized by ship and plane. They were decisive in repelling the invaders. By March 1976 the last South African troops were driven out.

Over the following decade, the apartheid regime and the imperialist-backed UNITA (National Union for the Total Independence of Angola) waged a bloody war against the Angolan government in which hundreds of thousands were killed, mostly civilians. Some 2,077 Cuban internationalists gave their lives during the mission.

In the second half of 1987, the Angolan army undertook an ill-conceived offensive against UNITA forces in the southeast, an isolated area far from resupply points and reinforcements. They did so following the guidance of Soviet military advisers, and against the advice of the Cuban leadership. The apartheid regime, seeing an opportunity to trap and annihilate the best Angolan units, sent large numbers of troops, tanks, and planes into Angola to back UNITA.

In response to Luanda's plea for help in face of this critical situation, Cuba's revolutionary leadership sent massive reinforcements of both troops and weapons. A counteroffensive was launched to bring the South African intervention to an end once and for all. The Cuban forces halted the assault on Cuito Cuanavale. Then, together with Angolan soldiers and combatants from Namibia's South West Africa People's Organisation (SWAPO), they attacked with overwhelming power in southwestern Angola, advancing almost to the Namibian border and for the first time gaining air superiority over the South African invaders.

Pretoria was dealt a resounding defeat. Forced to the negotiating table, South African officials agreed to the permanent withdrawal of their troops from Angola and accepted the independence of Namibia. The last Cuban troops left Angola in May 1991.

Workers and young people fighting to bring down apartheid

Angola, November 1987–April 1988

Arrows denote movement of Cuban-Angolan-SWAPO forces.

Cuban troop positions, November 1987.

Forward position of Cuban-Angolan-SWAPO troops, April 1988.

in South Africa were given a powerful boost. By 1994 the white-supremacist regime was toppled by a massive popular upsurge. African National Congress leader Nelson Mandela, imprisoned for 27 years, was elected president in 1994 in South Africa's first post-apartheid elections.

"The crushing defeat of the racist army at Cuito Cuanavale was a victory for the whole of Africa!" said Nelson Mandela during a visit to Cuba in 1991. "Cuito Cuanavale has been a turning point in the struggle to free the continent and our country from the scourge of apartheid!"[2]

■

WATERS: At various times between 1975 and 1991 all three of you served in Angola as part of Cuba's internationalist mission there. Can you tell us about this mission and its importance for Cuba and Africa?

CHUI: The Cuban Revolution has been true to the legacy of the internationalists who helped us in the war for independence and in other struggles since then. Generals Máximo Gómez, who was Dominican; Carlos Roloff, who was Polish; Luis Marcano, who was Dominican; Juan Rius Rivera, who was Puerto Rican—all fought for Cuba's independence.

CHOY: Henry Reeve, "El Inglesito."

CHUI: Yes, the "Little Englishman" who was actually American.

CHOY: And Thomas Jordan, another American, who had

2.   Mandela spoke on July 26, 1991, in Matanzas, Cuba, together with Fidel Castro. Both speeches appear in *How Far We Slaves Have Come! Cuba and South Africa in Today's World* (Pathfinder, 1991). See also Fidel Castro, Raúl Castro, and others, *Cuba and Angola: Fighting for Africa's Freedom and Our Own* (Pathfinder, 2013); and Harry Villegas, *Cuba and Angola: The War for Freedom* (Pathfinder, 2017).

fought in the US Civil War on the side of the Confederacy.

CHUI: Throughout our history there were many internationalists who fought for our freedom. We have been true to their legacy.

When we carry out missions in countries that request our assistance, we have the opportunity to do what they did.

We lent assistance to the Congo, for example, and to the Republic of Guinea when Sékou Touré was president. At various times we also aided Guinea-Bissau, Cape Verde, Somalia, Ethiopia, Algeria, Syria, Yemen, Oman, Sierra Leone, São Tomé and Príncipe, Benin, Equatorial Guinea, and other nations in Africa and the Middle East.[3]

In terms of the Americas, there's Nicaragua, Grenada, and Guyana, among others, including Venezuela today.

We should stress that this aid has been of every type. It includes medical, construction, educational, and cultural assistance as well as military missions.

SÍO WONG: Our people hold socialist and internationalist ideas. That's how we've been educated. What other country can provide four or five thousand doctors for voluntary internationalist work when asked for help? But not only doctors. Our soldiers. The 375,000 Cuban combatants who served in Angola between 1975 and 1991 were all volunteers. That may not be well known, but it's a fact.

Each one was asked: "Are you willing to participate?"

3. The story of some of these efforts is recounted in Ernesto Che Guevara, *Pasajes de la guerra revolucionaria: Congo* (published in English as *The African Dream*, New York: Grove Press, 2000); Víctor Dreke, *From the Escambray to the Congo* (Pathfinder, 2002); and the two-volume work by Piero Gleijeses, *Conflicting Missions: Havana, Washington, and Africa, 1959–1976* (Chapel Hill: University of North Carolina Press, 2002), and *Visions of Freedom: Havana, Washington, Pretoria, and the Struggle for Southern Africa, 1976–1991* (2013).

"No, my mother's sick," someone might answer.

"Then you don't go," he'd be told.

It was genuinely voluntary. This was one of the conditions established by the party and Fidel. How can you risk your life for a just cause unless it's voluntary? There's no other way it can be done.

The battle of Cuito Cuanavale

WATERS: Nelson Mandela called the 1987–88 battle of Cuito Cuanavale "a turning point in the history of Africa." Yet outside Cuba—and much of Africa—this battle is largely unknown.

SÍO WONG: In late 1987 the enemy almost completely surrounded a group of Cuban and Angolan troops at Cuito Cuanavale. And the decisive battle took place there. The battle lasted more than four months, and in March 1988 the South African army was defeated. That defeat marked the beginning of the end. It forced them to sit down at the negotiating table. And they accepted an agreement.

Otherwise the offensive would have continued . . .

CHUI: . . . which could have endangered their stability.

SÍO WONG: Yes. And their defeat had a whole series of consequences—including the independence of Namibia and the release of Mandela after twenty-seven years in prison.

CHUI: It "broke the back of the South African army," to use Fidel's words.

SÍO WONG: How is it possible that the South Africans, with all their military and economic might, were forced to sit down at the negotiating table? From a strategic point of view, what we carried out was a deterrence operation. Our strategy was to concentrate a mass of tanks in southern Angola. How many tanks were there, Chui? Five hundred, a thousand? You'd have to look up the exact figures. It was a deterrent

Apartheid regime broke its teeth at Cuito Cuanavale

In Cuito Cuanavale the South Africans really broke their teeth. And it all came about with a minimum of casualties—a minimum of casualties!—for our own forces, the Angolans and Cubans. . . .

The Cuban-Angolan strategy wasn't simply to stop the enemy at Cuito Cuanavale, but to gather enough forces and equipment on the western end of our lines to advance southward and threaten key positions of the South African forces. . . . Enough troops were gathered to seriously threaten points of strategic importance for South Africa and strike hard at them on terrain that we, and not the enemy, had chosen. . . .

A handful of pilots went on hundreds upon hundreds of missions in only a few weeks. They had control of the air with the MIG-23s, and we must say they carried out a great feat. That was an important factor.

We not only sent our best pilots to Angola. We also sent our best antiaircraft weapons, a large amount of portable antiaircraft equipment, a good quantity of antiaircraft missile artillery. We reinforced our air power and sent as many tanks, armored troop carriers, and artillery pieces as were needed. . . .

We did not give the enemy a single opportunity. Not a single opportunity! . . .

In this way the conditions were created that made possible the negotiations.

FIDEL CASTRO
DECEMBER 5, 1988

force, since it could have crossed into Namibia and continued southward.

The idea was always to do battle with the fewest possible casualties. How to accomplish that? Through superiority in the relationship of forces.

At one point in that operation our troop strength in Angola reached 50,000, equipped with artillery, tanks, and planes—80 percent of them deployed in the south. We built roads for our tanks and artillery. In just ten weeks we built an airstrip so our planes could provide cover for forces at the front, since the South Africans had a large number of aircraft. Up to that time, they had air superiority.

Leaders set the example

WATERS: Compañero Chui, what were your responsibilities related to the Angola campaign?

CHUI: Starting in September 1971 I was second in command of the 10th Directorate of the Revolutionary Armed Forces, the FAR's unit in charge of internationalist assistance. I served under Commander Raúl Díaz Argüelles, who had participated in Guinea-Bissau's war of liberation. In December 1975, barely a month after the start of our internationalist mission in Angola, Argüelles, who commanded our forces there, was killed by a mine, and I was named head of this directorate.

As Moisés mentioned earlier, I too had the honor of working under three leaders: Fidel, Raúl, and Almeida. I served under Almeida in the Sierra and am doing so again today in the Association of Combatants of the Cuban Revolution.

I served under Raúl in the Ministry of the Revolutionary Armed Forces from the time I was very young. He has educated and trained me. In the armed forces I was head of a number of bodies: Armaments, the 10th Directorate, and

Cadres. I was also deputy chief of staff.

And beginning in September 1975, for two years I had the honor of working together with Fidel and Raúl in the Special Command Post to lead our forces during the first phase of the internationalist assistance to the people of Angola. The command post of Operation Carlota, as it was known, directed the dispatch and deployment of forces—first our instructors and then our combat volunteers—as well as supplies.

I acquired a lot of experience, not to mention Fidel's knocking some sense into me from time to time. But that's how you learn, and that's how leadership cadres are trained.

KOPPEL: When were you in Angola?

CHUI: I was there briefly in 1976, and I later served from 1986 to 1988. As Mary-Alice said, Moisés, Choy, and I all served in Angola.

But not only that. The majority of the officers of the armed forces at that time took part in internationalist missions to one or more African countries. We gained experience in combat, troop organization, transport, and logistics. At times we did so together with the Soviets.

In 1977 I participated in establishing Cuba's military mission in Ethiopia, and I was also part of similar undertakings in Mozambique in 1977 and Nicaragua in 1979.

In 1986 I was named deputy chief of staff of the Cuban military mission in Angola, a responsibility I held until December 1987. At that time, on my request, I was named head of Operation 31st Anniversary—the reinforcement of Cuban troops and munitions for the battle of Cuito Cuanavale, which had begun in November. That operation was organized and directed by the commander in chief.

SÍO WONG: I'll tell you a story that says something about Fidel's leadership of the Angola mission. In 1984 or 1985 Fidel went to the Soviet Union to attend the funeral of the Com-

munist Party general secretary—I don't remember whether
it was Andropov or Chernenko.[4] The room was filled with
Soviet marshals and generals, who were wondering where
Fidel had studied strategy, operational arts, military science.
They had seen how Fidel directed the war in Angola and
were astounded by it. Even more so when FAR officers in our
delegation replied, with a smile, that Fidel had studied at the
military academy of the sierras.

To organize an operation of this scope 10,000 kilometers
away! And this wasn't a guerrilla operation. We were directing a regular war. How could a small country, without the
great resources of the Soviet Union or the United States, supply an operation at that distance? How could it defeat an army
such as South Africa's, along with the Zairean army and the
mercenaries?

Chui is a witness. He was in the command center where,
night after night, Fidel directed operations.

Fidel knew the terrain in Angola better even than those of
us who were over there. "Go to such-and-such river, at such-
and-such hill," he'd say in his cables. It was just like the Sierra
Maestra, which he knew like the back of his hand. "Go to the
top of such-and-such hill," he'd say. He would send a message to Che, to Ramiro [Valdés]: "Take such-and-such position." In Angola it was the same. He'd send a message to General Leopoldo Cintra Frías—Polo—who headed the military
mission during the final stage: "Polito, position three tanks
on such-and-such road. Don't let yourselves be outflanked."

WATERS: Numerous ranking Cuban officers gave their lives
in Angola. Chui mentioned Raúl Díaz Argüelles, his com-

4. Soviet Communist Party general secretary Yuri Andropov died in
    February 1984. He was replaced by Konstantin Chernenko, who
    died in March 1985.

mander and head of the mission in 1975. Raúl [Castro], in one of his tributes to those who fell in combat in Angola, noted that a quarter of them were officers. Chui, you yourself were seriously wounded. How did that happen?

CHUI: It was while my combat brigade was being transferred to Malanje province in northern Angola. On March 5, 1988, I was riding at the head of the third convoy, the one in which the weaponry was being transported. My vehicle set off a reinforced antitank mine, and I was thrown almost twenty meters. I was in critical condition.

Our commander in chief sent a plane to take me back to Cuba, given the gravity of my state. After quite a battle, medical science was able to save my life. But they had to amputate my right leg, which was in very bad shape. Typical of Fidel, he would ask about my health every day and gave precise instructions on what actions to take. I was treated first in the Brothers Ameijeiras Hospital by a very competent multidisciplinary team. Later, for my recuperation, I was transferred to the Center for Surgical Medicine Research, and I finished my rehabilitation at Carlos J. Finlay Military Hospital.

SÍO WONG: In our army the leader is an example. We believe this is very important. This is also true for the revolutionary cadre. It's part of our code of ethics for cadres. The leader has to set an example.

This was always a characteristic of Che, who was incapable of giving an order he himself was not prepared to carry out. And it's equally true of Raúl and Fidel.

During the revolutionary war, as I mentioned earlier, compañeros had to write to Fidel asking him not to participate in combat. The same went for Raúl in the Second Eastern Front. Because Fidel and Raúl frequently put themselves at risk in combat. That's one of the reasons people follow them. It's a quality that Raúl has inculcated in our military leaders.

They're first in combat, first in setting a personal example of austerity in the way they live.

The imperialists and counterrevolutionaries, including the Miami mafia types, have created a harsh and even blood-thirsty image of Raúl, but the truth is totally the opposite. I've known Raúl for more than forty years, seven of them working directly with him. He's a man of deep human sensibility. His entire life has been dedicated to fighting for the people. He's capable of attending to the country's most important problems while being attuned to the family and personal matters of individual compañeros and to what ordinary people face.

In private life, away from service, we're friends. I get together with his family, and sometimes my sister Angelita invites him over for a Chinese dinner. But at work he's the minister and I'm his subordinate. He's very straight with you and demanding.

That's why we've been able to organize armed forces with that discipline, devotion, dedication, prepared for anything. As Fidel has said publicly, Raúl is the organizer of a disciplined army, a proletarian army.

CHOY: Raúl demands discipline—the same discipline he himself has. You see it in the way he dresses. Sometimes he demands that a person put his cap on, or button his shirt. But he himself follows the dress code of the armed forces strictly. His uniform is always buttoned correctly.

Cuba's strategic mission

WATERS: During the time the Cuban volunteers were in Angola, you had to contend with UNITA, the Angolan force headed by Jonas Savimbi, which had South African and US backing. What was the approach of the Cuban armed forces toward UNITA?

SÍO WONG: We didn't participate directly in Angola's

struggle against the UNITA bandits led by Savimbi, who stood in the way of consolidating Angola's independence. We advised the Angolan armed forces, but we didn't participate in combat against UNITA.

We were there to help the Angolans, along with the Namibians, against South Africa's intervention, against aggression from the outside. Not to support any one of the groups within the country. It's important to state that clearly. We were very, very careful that our troops didn't directly participate in combat among Angolans.

Fidel has explained this numerous times. The strategic mission of our troops was to repel an invasion from South Africa and prevent an invasion from Zaire. We went no further than the border with Namibia. Internal problems must be resolved by those involved, by the belligerents themselves. That's always been our clear stand.

CHOY: We fought UNITA only when UNITA attacked us. Our strategic mission was to prevent an invasion by South Africa or Zaire that would destroy the revolutionary, nationalist, independence process in Angola.

CHUI: Civil wars are very cruel. Citizens of the same nationality, even family members fighting against each other.

SÍO WONG: We also had to be very careful because, as Chui said, the Angolans had Soviet advisers as well as our own. It was very complex.

We had many arguments with Soviet military leaders concerning the structuring of the popular armed forces of Angola. Because their thinking and our thinking ran in two totally different directions. The Soviets were for creating large divisions, tank brigades, a classical army. But in our high command, Fidel insisted that the Angolans needed light units, not large units. That the forest wouldn't accommodate big tank units.

In case of foreign invasion, we were there with small tactical groups. They were composed of an infantry unit, a tank unit, artillery, antiaircraft defense, designed to move very rapidly, with great maneuverability.

Moreover, we knew through our intelligence that the South Africans had seven tactical nuclear weapons. We had to take that into account. The Americans knew this too but permitted the South Africans to have them. A nuclear weapon wipes out a large unit at one blow. We had to have small units that would not be as vulnerable.

CHUI: We had to take into account the length of supply lines, too. Provisioning these smaller units wasn't as massive a job.

SÍO WONG: So we had long arguments with the Soviets, and we never came to an agreement. But time proved us right.

Negotiations with South Africa

KOPPEL: Choy, when were you in Angola?

CHOY: I served in Angola in 1980–81. I was deputy head of our Anti-Aircraft Defense and Air Force there. The commander in chief and the minister of the FAR also assigned me to work with my Angolan counterparts to organize Angola's antiaircraft defense and air force.

This wasn't an easy task, since it involved very close coordination with the Soviets. The Soviets sent the weapons and we sent the personnel.

KOPPEL: What did you do after returning from Angola?

CHOY: When I got back to Cuba in 1981, I held various leadership posts in the Anti-Aircraft Defense and Revolutionary Air Force (DAAFAR).

In December 1986 the Council of State named me ambassador to Cape Verde, a position I held until 1992. During that time, on Sal Island, which is part of the Cape Verde Islands, the agreement with the South Africans was reached follow-

ing their defeat in the battle of Cuito Cuanavale. The govern-
mental accord was signed later at the United Nations in New
York, but the basic agreement was achieved at Sal Island on
July 27, 1988, between the South African, Angolan, and Cuban delegations. The essence of the agreement was that the
South Africans would pull out of Angola for good, provided
that Cuban armored units halted our advance before reaching the Namibian border and pulled back to a line north of
the Cunene River, in southern Angola.

On the very day the Sal Island proposal was reached, the
vanguard of General Enrique Acevedo's tank brigade, which
was the forward detachment, had crossed the Cunene River.
Behind it were a number of other brigades. We were practically at the Namibian border. The South Africans were in
shock at this turn of events. There's an anecdote from the Sal
Island negotiations.

As I mentioned, the South Africans had stated their willingness to leave Angola for good if Cuban military units
stopped our march toward the Namibian border and returned to a line north of the Cunene River. The South Africans set the line. When the Cuban military delegation studied
that line, they realized it was very close to the river. When it
rained the area turned into a swamp, and the tanks wouldn't
be able to move from there, posing the real danger that hundreds of these armored vehicles could become sitting ducks
in case the war resumed. So our delegation offered to set a
line even farther away from the Namibian border.

When this offer was made, the South African response
was: "The Cubans aren't so bad after all!"

There was a second meeting at Sal Island a year or so later
to review the implementation of the agreement. The South
African delegation at that second meeting was headed by
first vice minister of foreign relations, Neil Van Heerden,

who dealt with the Angola question for them, plus four of their generals. Our delegation included General Cintra Frías and me.

The South Africans first tried to bribe us. Van Heerden began by explaining that South Africa was devoting 500 million rand [US$200 million at the time] annually to "sustaining" Namibia. He said they were ready to continue giving Namibia this money provided there was peace at the border. What did that mean? That there would be no support for the African National Congress (ANC) and other movements in South Africa. They were practically asking us to commit a betrayal, in other words, and to pressure SWAPO [South-West African People's Organisation of Namibia] to betray the antiapartheid struggle in South Africa. Of course, the political leadership of our country didn't agree.

At one point in the meeting, the head of our delegation, Carlos Aldana, turned to Cintra Frías and said, "General, please tell Mr. Van Heerden how much weaponry we've withdrawn."

Polo gave the number of men, artillery pieces, and tanks—800 of them.

Van Heerden's mouth dropped.

He knew that even after that withdrawal, thousands of artillery pieces, tanks, other motorized vehicles, and men still remained with our forces in southern Angola.

"And what are you going to do in Cuba with so many tanks and so much artillery?" Van Heerden asked.

"They'll probably go to the Territorial Troop Militia" was our response.[5]

His mouth was still open. Clearly the South Africans would have been unable to stand up to that force advancing toward the Namibian border.

5. See glossary, Territorial Troop Militia.

WATERS: General Sío Wong, what were your duties?

SÍO WONG: I served in Angola in 1976. I was logistics chief for the military mission—a mission 10,000 kilometers away carried out by a small country.

I remember reading an article in the US press, I think it was the *New York Times,* reporting that the US government was shocked at the operation we had carried out. It spoke about the extraordinary logistical support, saying Cuban soldiers in the trenches didn't lack even for Havana Club rum. That was a lie, of course. Maybe they were thinking about how US soldiers get their holiday turkey, their ice cream, and so on.

Support, yes. The combatants need a certain minimum of logistical support. We were able to do that because we are a socialist country. Within the bounds of our material limitations, all the resources necessary were made available.

All of Cuba behind Angola effort

You've got to give credit to the courage of compañeros who boarded the old Britannias. By the mid-1970s, when the Angolan mission began, those obsolete four-motor prop planes were practically out of service. We installed some additional fuel tanks so they could reach Sal Island off the coast of West Africa. They first had to make a stop in Guyana, then on Sal Island. So the trip to Angola by the first instructors was done in three legs. To fly in those Britannias you had to be brave, willing to risk your life. Later the Soviets approved the use of IL-62 planes for a number of flights, to transport some of our troops. There were ten flights during the early stages of the mission, I recall. I was on one of them.

We used our merchant fleet to transport thousands of troops and large amounts of combat matériel. It was a secret operation utilizing a number of ports. This could only have been done by a country like Cuba, with that type of spirit of solidarity.

I repeat: for these internationalist missions, we put the entire country behind the effort. Because we felt it was for something vital.

No, we didn't send bottles of Havana Club, but we did assure the essentials. We maintained a 10,000-kilometer supply line. That's something done by powerful countries such as the United States and Russia, countries with vast air and naval fleets. The US military, for instance, draws up contingency plans for its forces to wage wars on two fronts at the same time. They have the weaponry to do so. They have the supplies, the logistics.

As the one who headed logistics, I took a direct personal interest in the *New York Times* article I mentioned. But the effort was accomplished only because the entire country was mobilized behind it, with the goal of maintaining supplies for the troops. This chapter in our history has not yet been fully recorded, but it was a real feat.

From the human side, our troops went to Angola as part of an internationalist mission. That, too, was part of the anonymous work carried out by our people. They didn't ask where someone was being sent, nor could we tell them. A regiment would embark from the port of Nuevitas in Camagüey. So a story would circulate to the effect that the Havana regiment was going on maneuvers at the FAR's national live-fire range. The regiment would embark at night, in secret. It traveled without an escort. The vessel could easily have been sunk. Imagine a ship carrying a thousand soldiers that could easily have been attacked by a high-speed pirate vessel firing a bazooka blast. We were running a risk. That's why it had to be secret.

Someday the military academies will have to study this. How was it possible? Clearly it was the participation of the entire people.

CHUI: A base of support for this effort existed among the general population. That's without a doubt. The people could see the leadership vision that was being demonstrated. They had confidence in Fidel as a leader. Even though the battlefield was in Angola, they understood perfectly the instructions coming from here in Cuba. And they followed them.

A turning point in history of Africa

KOPPEL: In the United States people know very little about what the Cuban Revolution has done to aid anti-imperialist struggles in Angola and elsewhere in Africa. But there will be a lot of interest in learning about this.

CHUI: We were a decisive factor during the 1970s in winning the independence of the Portuguese empire's three major colonies on that continent—Angola, Mozambique, and Guinea-Bissau and the Cape Verde Islands. Nevertheless, these facts aren't stressed very much.

In the case of Guinea-Bissau, for example, the PAIGC [African Party for the Independence of Guinea-Bissau and Cape Verde] led by Amilcar Cabral requested Cuban aid in fighting for the independence of their country. And our troops played an important part in the defeat of the Portuguese army, leading to the liberation of most of Guinea-Bissau by 1973. That event shook the Portuguese government, contributing to the "Carnation Revolution" in 1974. From this came a "domino effect" with the independence of Angola, Mozambique, and São Tomé and Príncipe.[6]

6. The Portuguese dictatorship was toppled in April 1974 (see glossary, Portuguese revolution). Mozambique obtained its independence in June 1975. São Tomé and Príncipe became independent in July 1975; Angola in November 1975.

Choy knows this history well from the time he spent as ambassador in Cape Verde.

The case of Angola merits special attention. Our troops remained there fighting together with the Angolan people for more than fifteen years. Not only did we help defeat the South African army, but we also helped bring about the elimination of apartheid and the independence of Namibia.

From our efforts in Africa, the Cubans brought back nothing material for Cuba. Only our wounded and dead, and the satisfaction of a duty fulfilled.

sío wong: History demonstrated we were right. We were not fighting just for Angola. From a strategic point of view, we were fighting against apartheid. And indeed at Cuito Cuanavale, after we broke the back of the apartheid army, they had to come to the negotiating table, grant independence to Namibia, free Nelson Mandela, and accelerate the process that soon led to the destruction of the apartheid system itself.

Angola strengthened Cuban Revolution

waters: What was the impact on Cuba itself? Not everyone agreed with expending such resources, with staying the course for so many years. Did the internationalist mission in Angola strengthen the Cuban Revolution?

choy: Well, it really strengthened us from an ideological standpoint. All of us who went had studied slavery, the exploitation of man by man, the exploitation of the countries in southern Africa. We had studied the evils that colonialism had wrought and was still creating. But we'd merely read about it in books.

In my own case—and I'm sure the same thing happened to other Cubans—I got there and could see with my own eyes what the colonial system really was. A complete differentiation between the whites, the Europeans—in this case

Ours was a revolutionary army of the people

The Cuban presence in Angola was the continuation of the best traditions of our nation. If there was anything unusual about it, it was the people's massive participation, which had never before reached such levels, which unleashed the will of an entire people to take part in the epic struggle. Even more far-reaching and significant was the absolutely voluntary nature of their participation.

Ours was not just a professional army, even if we take great pride in our troops' performance in combat and technical training. It was an army of the masses, a revolutionary army of the people. . . .

As we pledged at the start, we didn't bring back with us anything other than the satisfaction of fulfilling our duty and the remains of our fallen comrades. . . .

In the course of this extraordinary test, a decisive role was played by the commanders and officers who bore the brunt of countless decisions. They were called upon, above all, to set an example. And indeed they did so to the hilt, as evidenced by the fact that one of every four of our men killed in action was an officer. . . .

When we face new and unexpected challenges, we will always be able to recall the epic of Angola with gratitude, because without Angola we would not be as strong as we are today.

If our people know themselves better, if we know much better what all of us are capable of achieving—

(Continued on next page)

> veterans as well as our young people, the new genera-
> tions—that, too, is thanks to Angola. . . .
> If today we are more aware of the work of the revolu-
> tion, because we have experienced the disastrous re-
> mains of colonialism and underdevelopment, for that
> we must thank Angola.
>
> RAÚL CASTRO
> *MAY 27, 1991*

the Portuguese—and the native population. We saw how
these countries were exploited. We saw a country that was
so rich, yet Angolans were living in what we saw as subhuman conditions. Because their country's riches were being
stolen. Because the colonialists had not preserved the forests
or the land.

Sometimes we'd be traveling in vehicles, and people walking along the road would run when they heard us coming.
We learned why. Under Portuguese rule, if the native inhabitants didn't get out of the way, the colonialists would sometimes run them over. This went on for generations. So whenever they heard a vehicle coming, they'd run. And not just
off to the shoulder of the road either. They ran because they'd
been mistreated like this for years, for centuries.

The main lesson I learned from this mission was to fully
appreciate colonialism's cruelty toward the native population
and the naked theft of their natural resources. To see a country with great natural wealth like Angola, yet with a population facing needs of the most basic type!

That's why I say that knowing the truth strengthened us
politically. The same thing happens whenever we see how a
layer of the population in capitalist countries lacks the most

Cuban people made a contribution unparalleled in African history

The Cuban people hold a special place in the hearts of the people of Africa. The Cuban internationalists have made a contribution to African independence, freedom, and justice, unparalleled for its principled and selfless character. From its earliest days the Cuban Revolution has itself been a source of inspiration to all freedom-loving people. . . .

What other country can point to a record of greater selflessness than Cuba has displayed in its relations with Africa?

How many countries of the world benefit from Cuban health workers or educationists? How many of these are in Africa?

Where is the country that has sought Cuban help and has had it refused? How many countries under threat from imperialism or struggling for national liberation have been able to count on Cuban support?

It was in prison when I first heard of the massive assistance that the Cuban internationalist forces provided to the people of Angola, on such a scale that one hesitated to believe, when the Angolans came under combined attack of South African, CIA-financed FNLA, mercenary, UNITA, and Zairean troops in 1975.

We in Africa are used to being victims of countries wanting to carve up our territory or subvert our sovereignty. It is unparalleled in African history to have another people rise to the defense of one of us.

NELSON MANDELA, MATANZAS, CUBA
JULY 26, 1991

basic necessities. The first time I went to Madrid, for instance, it was December. It's cold there that time of year. On the Gran Vía, the main street of that large city, I saw people sleeping on the sidewalk near a heating vent, with bags and newspapers over them.

You read about things like that in books, and you believe they're true. But until you see them for yourself, you can't fully understand the reality Karl Marx wrote about. That, I believe, is one of the lessons we all learned from internationalist missions.

These are the same lessons our doctors have learned, our athletic trainers, and other specialists who go to many countries. This includes countries that have natural riches yet suffer tremendous backwardness and have great contrasts. The resources aren't used to help the masses of the people. And such backwardness isn't only in Africa. It's in the Americas too.

Bolivia, for example, has many tin mines. It has oil and natural gas. Nonetheless, it's tremendously backward. Ecuador the same, even though it's one of the principal exporters of oil. There are permanent social problems, because much of the population lives in virtually subhuman conditions. Until you see these realities, you don't understand how deep the problem goes. You don't understand what the people need. Direct contact with these problems strengthens our understanding. Those missions made this understanding concrete.

On diplomatic missions, you see this same reality from a different angle. I was able to see the kind of pressure Washington and other imperialist powers bring to bear on these countries.

Once I was talking about something to Cape Verde's secretary of state for cooperation, the equivalent of a deputy foreign minister. He was a good person with whom we had good relations. "The US ambassador spoke to me about this very problem," he told me, "and threatened that if our position was such and such, they would cut our economic aid." You read about things like this, but it's different when you hear them yourself. I had the chance to observe this when I was a diplomat. You can't speak out about these things publicly sometimes. I thought the Cape Verdeans should have made a statement, but they didn't. And these were friendly countries. But they avoided speaking publicly about something that would clash with US interests.

That's how it was.

CHUI: As Choy was saying, this experience helped all of us develop politically and ideologically. But the biggest impact was among the soldiers. In Angola and other countries of Africa, they could fully grasp the illiteracy, the misery, the lack of education, the lack of sanitary conditions and health care—conditions that people continue to live under.

Let me tell you a story. One time we slaughtered a pig, and I told one of the Cuban soldiers to give a piece of the leg to the Angolans. The Angolans said no, they didn't want it. When we asked why, they said they wanted the viscera, the innards. That's what the colonial masters always used to give them, and they had developed a taste for it. They really didn't like anything else. They weren't used to it.

Our internationalist combatants observed what people in these countries lack, things we don't lack in Cuba. They learned, in general, a whole series of lessons, and acquired valuable experiences about the inequalities and injustices of today's world.

There are many in the world who denigrate our stance of helping the peoples of other countries who are fighting imperialist oppression. But within Cuba it enabled us to consolidate the political and ideological development of the young people who went to fight and to assist other peoples, who understood the justice of their cause and were later proud of their mission. You couldn't find a better example of this than the Five Heroes being held prisoner by the empire because of the internationalist mission they were carrying out to defend the people of Cuba against terrorist attacks. They are part of this generation, and three of them served in Angola.[7]

SÍO WONG: On top of the things the compañeros have described, you have to add what our young doctors experience when they go to other countries. It sickens them. They see patients die before their eyes because the person doesn't have money. That's something that doesn't happen in Cuba. Such life experience means more than a hundred classes from a manual on Marxism. It's tremendous training for young people.

Right now we don't have any internationalist combat missions. We have other kinds of missions—as doctors, teachers, and more. But the simple fact that compañeros go and live in a capitalist country has a profound impact. This is something the three of us lived through growing up. But it's not something our young people today have experienced.

You can say many things to your children about what the past was like. When I was young, I recall, my brothers and sisters would tell me about the Machado dictatorship in the 1930s. They'd tell me about the big economic crisis of those years. But it's not the same as when you see, feel, live it yourself. If someone says, "Capitalism is like this; capitalism is like that," it's not the same thing. No, go live it. This is an experience for all our young people, because those who go—doctors, teachers, technicians, specialists—convey it to all members of their families.

7.   See glossary, Cuban Five.

WATERS: Did the internationalist mission in Angola have an impact on Cuba's defense preparedness?

SÍO WONG: I wanted to talk about that aspect too, about how useful this was for us. More than 300,000 Cubans got actual combat experience in Angola. That's something the Pentagon has to take into account when they make their analyses.

Certain things are now being declassified, such as some of the previously top secret documents from the October Crisis of 1962. They reveal quite concretely how US leaders weigh their decisions. Kennedy asked the Pentagon chiefs how many casualties they would suffer in an invasion of Cuba, and they told him the estimate was 18,000 in the first ten days. The price would be very high. Very costly.[8]

During the October Crisis, as the commander in chief said, no one trembled or flinched. Our people are quite willing and ready, quite firm and determined.

That's what the Pentagon has to take into consideration.

8. This episode is described in *Making History*. Also see glossary, Cuban "Missile" Crisis (October Crisis).

War of the entire people

WATERS: General Sío Wong, the assignment you've had for nearly twenty years—president of Cuba's National Institute of State Reserves—is closely tied to Cuba's defense. Can you explain what the reserves are?

SÍO WONG: The National Institute of State Reserves (INRE) was established in 1981. During the 1960s and 1970s the government had put aside reserves for wartime or other emergencies. And the FAR had its own reserves. By the end of the 1970s, however, we recognized the need to systematically increase these reserves and to create a body that would take charge of directing and overseeing them.

INRE's task is to accumulate material resources to guarantee the economy's normal development and functioning in peacetime, to prevent disasters or attenuate their consequences, and to strengthen the country's defense capacities.

WATERS: You said INRE was formed in 1981. US threats against Cuba were escalating then because of Cuba's solidarity with the new workers and farmers governments in Grenada and Nicaragua.

SÍO WONG: Yes, INRE was formed right at the time US policy toward those revolutions hardened. Reagan had just become president. The Soviets had already told us we weren't under

a nuclear umbrella. Raúl has explained this publicly.[9]
That's when we changed our military doctrine. We adopted
the policy of the war of the entire people. That is, we defend
ourselves with our own forces and means, based on each
man, and each woman too, having a weapon—a rifle, a mine,
a rock, something to fight the enemy with.

Our first reserve is the Territorial Troop Militia, founded
in 1980 but whose origins date back to the Revolutionary National Militia created in 1959. In addition, a large part of the
population is organized in Production and Defense Brigades.

Many friends point out that we didn't sign the treaty
against antipersonnel mines. López Cuba explained it very
well in *Making History*. Antipersonnel mines are the weapons
of the poor. We have neither rockets nor atomic weapons. We
have to defend ourselves. Moreover, mines are a defensive
weapon, purely defensive.[10]

WATERS: And the State Reserves are a weapon of defense
as well?

SÍO WONG: One purpose of organizing the reserves is precisely to strengthen the country's capacity to defend itself. We
hope we won't be forced to use them in wartime. The best way
to win a war is to prevent it. To prevent it we have to be strong.

9. In an April 21, 1993, interview with *El Sol de México*, Raúl Castro recounted how in 1981 he had met with top Soviet leaders, including
Communist Party general secretary Leonid Brezhnev, to discuss
responding to escalating US threats. The Soviet leadership explicitly told Castro that they were not willing to defend Cuba against
US attack. "We cannot fight in Cuba because you are 11,000 kilometers away from us," Castro reported Brezhnev telling him. "Do
you think we're going to go all that way to stick our necks out for
you?" The interview was also published in *Granma* in April 1993,
and in English in *Granma International*, May 5, 1993.

10. Interview with Division General Nestor López Cuba, *Making History*.

If we were to mark a moment that demonstrated these defense preparations, it was the Bastión 2004 strategic exercise held in December of that year.[11] The entire country participated. Hundreds of thousands mobilized on the final day of the exercise, which lasted almost a week. It had been nearly a decade since such an exercise had been organized in Cuba. I think the last one was in 1996. Bastión 2004 was led by Fidel, the commander in chief, as president of the Council of National Defense. It proved our people, our country, are prepared to confront any aggression.

We've studied the US wars against Yugoslavia in 1999 and Iraq in 2003, and our people's preparation was intensified in order to strengthen the country's defense capacities. US doctrine is to use technology and military power—air and rocketry—to bring their adversary to its knees with the minimum number of casualties to US forces. That's what they did in Yugoslavia. That's what they were trying to do in Iraq too.[12] They thought they could make it a "cakewalk."

During the war in Yugoslavia the US armed forces used their air power to bring the Yugoslav government to its knees in eighty days. If it had been possible to hold out another few weeks, world opinion would have continued shifting against the bombing. The Pentagon was analyzing what it would take to carry out an invasion. They knew a particular characteristic of Yugoslavia—that during World War II Tito's partisans fortified the mountains and in later years the country continued improving its defenses. We've sent military delegations there to study the Yugoslav defense system. All the necessary reserves are in underground tunnels in the

11. Bastión strategic exercises have continued to be held in December every four years.

12. See glossary, Iraq war (2003); and Yugoslavia, US-led war against.

mountains. So the eighty days of US bombings didn't affect even 1 percent of the Yugoslav military capability. NATO and the Pentagon came up with estimates as to the number of casualties they would sustain in the event of a land war. That's what they wanted to avoid. In the end, in any war you have to occupy territory on the ground.

Some callously referred to the US assault as a television war. "Today we're going to bomb the thermoelectric plant, tomorrow this or that bridge," and so on. But with that they broke the political will of the Yugoslav government to resist.

That wouldn't happen in Cuba. Our people are not divided. And here our generals can't be bought, as happened in Iraq. Open a Swiss bank account and buy off the generals. The troops don't fight.

It's not that the imperialists can't bomb us, or invade us. In Vietnam the war lasted more than ten years. The US had 58,000 of its troops killed. The resistance of the Vietnamese people made it possible to mobilize a powerful movement against the war within the United States itself. Eventually the US rulers were forced to withdraw from Vietnam.

In case of an attack against Cuba, in just one year's time— that is, about a tenth of the time the Vietnam War lasted— the US would suffer a minimum of 10,000 troops killed. That's the calculation we've made based on the preparation achieved by the Revolutionary Armed Forces and the people of Cuba, demonstrated by Bastión 2004. Among the people of the United States, opposition to the war would grow, as it did during Vietnam.

But to resist you must have reserves. To force the imperialists to decide whether they're going to fight on the ground and take the casualties that will affect support for the war— to do that, you must have reserves.

Our most important reserves are the patriotic reserves

of our people. But we must also have material reserves. We are an island. We can be blockaded easily. That's what the US government did during the "Missile" Crisis of October 1962. Under such circumstances, what quantity of oil would be needed? What quantity of food to feed 11 million inhabitants? We can't depend on foreign oil, on the contingencies of the world market.

All countries have reserves. But the country that has the greatest assortment of items in its reserves is Cuba. Not just fuel, lubricants, food, medicines, and raw materials. But even paper and pencils, so schools can remain open.

There is a decree of the president of the Council of State in which Fidel defines our policy on the reserves. In the first "whereas" he says: "The increase, preservation, and monitoring of the material reserves is an indispensable condition for the security of the nation, for feeding the population, and for the people's well-being."

That is the role of the reserves. That is what Fidel was explaining in January 2005 at the international economists conference when he talked about Cuba being militarily invulnerable and of working toward becoming economically invulnerable.

WATERS: Two broad economic and social challenges that are receiving considerable leadership attention are the problems in the electrical generating system and the effects of the unprecedented drought in several of Cuba's eastern provinces. These are strategic questions too, not unrelated to the reserves and Cuba's capacity to defend itself. Can you describe what you're dealing with?

SÍO WONG: Our national electrical grid was designed more than forty years ago. The system was the product of the favorable relations we had with the Soviet Union at the time. All the oil, the spare parts, the cables, the technology, everything, came from the Soviet Union. But to keep running, anything produced with Soviet technology had to have an oil tank attached. Plus a planeload of fuel for backup. Cars, trucks, tractors—everything was the same.

The entire electrical generation system is based on seven main thermoelectric plants that are interlinked. But that means the system is very vulnerable. If one plant fails it has serious repercussions for the whole system. Last year the turbine shaft of the Antonio Guiteras plant in Matanzas broke down. That is our most modern and efficient plant, built with French technology. We had to dismantle the shaft, contract for a plane, and send it to Mexico for repairs. With this plant's 350 megawatts offline, the whole system was destabilized.

Contributing to the electricity crisis has been a lengthening of the downtime for repair and maintenance. Since the beginning of the Special Period,[13] we've increasingly used crude oil extracted here in Cuba to generate electricity. This has saved us millions. But this oil has a high sulfur content. It doesn't burn as cleanly, which means more downtime for maintenance.

The nuclear-powered generators we were building in Juraguá on Cienfuegos Bay were intended to complement this system, reducing its vulnerability. A second thermonuclear plant was planned for Holguín. The nuclear plants were to augment and eventually replace much of the current system. This was the plan. But the Juraguá complex was a joint project with the Soviets, and in 1991 the Soviet Union fell.[14]

13. See glossary, Special Period. For more on Special Period, see part III.

14. Work on the Juraguá thermonuclear plant was begun in 1983, with Soviet collaboration. Following the collapse of the Soviet Union in

More than $1 billion had already been invested in the project. In order to complete it, another billion would have been necessary. Russia was not going to invest any more. We ourselves were not in a position to do so.

And there was another issue as well. Who were we going to depend on for nuclear fuel? Yeltsin? Putin?

We had no alternative. We decided to halt the work.

Fidel has outlined some of the steps we're taking to deal with the electricity crisis.[15] Cuba has doubled the amount of hard currency reserves to be invested in this area in 2005. Generators and equipment worth more than $280 million are currently being installed, which will give us a million more kilowatts of electricity within a year. The plan is to employ smaller and more efficient generators, spreading them more broadly throughout the country and thereby preventing the loss of electricity due to transmission over long distances. Doing so will also protect against damages to the national electrical system and power cuts due to hurricanes, which hit us every year.

The increased electricity generated by this newly installed equipment will be supplemented by 500,000 kilowatts generated by a new plant just finished in the eastern region, and by increasing the number of generating plants using natural gas that is a by-product of our crude oil production for fuel. Combined with measures to reduce energy consumption—like distributing new, more efficient pressure cookers and fans, repairing refrigerator door seals and thermostats, and exchanging incandescent

---

1991, the project was mothballed. In 1997 Fidel Castro announced that there were no plans to revive work on the Juraguá reactor.

15. Castro's speech of July 26, 2005, in which he indicated some of these steps, was printed in English in *Granma International*, July 31, 2005.

light bulbs for energy-saving ones—these changes will effectively double the electricity available for production, services, and domestic consumption by the second half of 2006.

But that's the legacy we're dealing with today and why the problems are so great.

WATERS: And the drought?

SÍO WONG: This is the worst drought Cuba has ever recorded, hitting the provinces of Holguín, Las Tunas, and Camagüey above all. More than two and a half million people have been affected at the most critical times. We've had to distribute water by truck to two million people, and to livestock as well. Camagüey is an area where there are large cattle ranches.

Despite the shortages of material resources, we've decided we have no choice. We have to go ahead with building two large water systems, plus the piping to transport water to the affected areas. This is a gigantic undertaking. One of these projects in the central part of the island was started before the Special Period, but work on it was halted due to lack of resources, fuel, machinery, and so on. Now it's going forward again. It will carry water from the center of the country to Camagüey. The other project will begin in the eastern mountains where the most rain falls, in the Moa region. There we'll start building several dams. The system of piping, canals, and tunnels will carry water to Holguín, Las Tunas, and all the way to Camagüey.

These are enormous undertakings, and they will have a very great economic impact.

WATERS: The reserves have been important in confronting the intensified economic war against Cuba waged by the US government the last decade and a half, haven't they?

SÍO WONG: Many compañeros don't realize how the US government's economic blockade affects us.[16]

When I was young I lived near Havana's Malecón, the boulevard along the seafront. I used to see the US ferries that came and went every day, transporting merchandise. At that time our trade was overwhelmingly with the United States.

In recent years, we've spoken with US congressmen from the South, and from other agricultural areas. In the National Assembly we received a delegation that included members of Congress from Louisiana. Before the triumph of the revolution, 36 percent of New Orleans's port trade was with Havana. You can imagine all the rice, corn, wheat, and oil we used to import from there. Now we import these items from places like Vietnam, China, and Malaysia. We even have to import powdered milk from New Zealand. We buy wheat in France. But the United States is just ninety miles away.

The blockade has cost us more than $80 billion in losses to our economy, just counting shipping and price differentials, and similar costs.[17]

'A leader who has no reserves is a bad leader'

KOPPEL: When did you become president of the National Institute of State Reserves?

16. Washington has maintained an embargo on trade to Cuba since February 1962. With the 1992 Cuban Democracy Act (the "Torricelli law") and the 1996 Cuban Liberty and Democratic Solidarity Act (the "Helms-Burton law"), the embargo was significantly tightened in an attempt to deepen the economic crisis resulting from the collapse of trade relations with the former Soviet Union and Eastern Europe. As of December 2017 neither of these laws nor any of their provisions have been rescinded.

17. Damages to the nation's economy from the more than fifty-year embargo total more than $800 billion, the Cuban government reported to the United Nations in November 2017.

SÍO WONG: I've carried that responsibility since 1986. But it's not the first time I've done something similar. During the revolutionary war, Fidel made me head of the Rebel Army's reserves for a time. Even then he called them the "strategic reserves."

"You're head of the reserves," he said. "Get to it."

We were keeping the strategic reserves in a little cave back then at the command post in La Plata. They consisted of ten 325-pound sacks of unrefined sugar, five cartons of condensed milk, and five boxes of canned sausages.

Some time later, Fidel came by after having toured the front for a week.

"So how's it going?" he asked. "How are the reserves?"

"There are six sacks left, commander."

"Six? How can that be? There were ten."

"Well, so-and-so came by. He didn't have anything to eat. And then what's-his-name arrived. And later someone else passed through with his platoon. They didn't have anything to eat, so I gave them a little sugar."

"Damn it," he exclaimed. "I put you in charge of the reserves, but you had no authority to give out a thing! Not even a spoonful of sugar."

He never said another word to me about the sugar. A few days later, however, Celia Sánchez brought me a handwritten note by Fidel. "Moisés," it said, "turn the reserves over to Otero. From now on you will concern yourself solely with the distribution of meat. Fidel."

I had been removed from my post and given a fictitious one; in those days we didn't have any meat to distribute!

I recalled this in 1986 when I was summoned to the offices of the Central Committee and informed that the Political Bureau had approved my nomination as president of the National Institute of State Reserves.

"Minister," I said to Raúl, "I was the first head of the strategic reserves, in the Sierra Maestra." I related the story of how I had headed up the reserves in the Sierra Maestra and been removed by Fidel. Then I said, "Tell the commander in chief that he may well be able to remove me for incompetence, for not doing my job well, for some mistake. But he won't be able to remove me for unauthorized use of the reserves." The commander in chief is the only one who authorizes their use. I'd learned my lesson.

When I returned to my office at the Ministry of the Revolutionary Armed Forces, I began to realize what those ten 325-pound sacks of sugar had represented. One gram of sugar has 4 calories. A glass of sugar water has 1,200 calories. With that you'll lose weight but you won't die. And with those reserves, the 200 men in the Sierra Maestra at the time could have gone for almost two months without getting anything from the outside. That's when I fully understood the importance of always having a reserve.

There's a saying that captures a deep truth: "A leader who has no reserves is not a good leader."

WATERS: How has the Special Period affected the reserves?

SÍO WONG: During the period when most of our supplies came from the socialist camp—from the Soviet Union primarily—there was not much consciousness of the need for reserves.

When we set up INRE in 1981, we did a whole number of studies, with the help of the USSR. Different opinions existed on the role and place of this body, as well as who it should work under. Initially it was attached to the State Committee of Technical-Material Supplies (CEATM). At the end of 1985, given the inadequate attention being paid to development of the reserves, it was decided to separate off INRE from CEATM and to put it directly under the president of the

Council of Ministers, Fidel.

I call that initial period the "lost decade." On the part of various bodies and officials there was a lack of consciousness about the importance of having reserves to confront any eventuality. Despite the instructions of the commander in chief and the calls of the minister of the FAR, it was necessary to wage a tremendous battle around this task. Before the Special Period there were many officials who argued: "If we don't have enough to eat, how can we put aside reserves?"

The Special Period showed that we had been wasting resources and that we could have accumulated a larger reserve. It also demonstrated the reserves' strategic importance.

The State Reserves enabled us to have fuel, to prevent the paralysis of basic economic functions like the sugar harvest, agriculture, and industry; food, to guarantee the basic ration; medicines, to save lives and prevent a single hospital from closing; even pencils and notebooks, to keep schools open.

We've advanced during the Special Period. But there's still a long way to go.

We don't use donations that come from all over the world as part of the reserve, although they're used by the government. The Cuban Institute for Friendship with the Peoples (ICAP) and the Ministry of Foreign Investment and Collaboration are responsible for keeping track of the receipt and distribution of donations.

A good example of why we have the reserves is Hurricane Michelle, which struck Cuba in November 2001. We were able to repair all the hurricane damage, and we did it in less than a year. Because we could count on a reserve of fuel, food, construction materials, roofs, power poles and cables, and so on. We were able to deal with the damage to 160,000 homes in seven provinces, 13,000 of them totally destroyed.

In July 2005 Hurricane Dennis battered ten provinces, damaging more than 175,000 homes, among them 28,000 completely destroyed, with total losses reaching $1.4 billion. It's the most destructive hurricane our country has faced since 1959. It was a Category 5 storm, the maximum on the Saffir-Simpson scale. The force of its winds reached more than 300 kilometers [185 miles] per hour. Some of the mountains in eastern Cuba suffered ecological damage that will take fifty years to heal.

In contrast to Cuba's approach, we've seen the consequences of natural disasters in countries far richer than we are, with much greater resources. A while back I was reading an article about relief claims made by people in Florida who had been affected by Hurricane Andrew, I believe. Andrew hit there in 1992—the "storm of the century," they call it—and people are still waiting for claims to be settled. They haven't received aid promised by the US government more than a decade ago!

But within a year after Hurricane Michelle we had repaired everything. And since agriculture was also hit, we supplied an additional quantity of rice, grain, and oil to those provinces that were affected. That's the way we respond to any natural disaster. That's what we are doing now to deal with the damages inflicted by Dennis.

PART III

The Special Period and beyond

Responding to food shortages during economic crisis of 1990s, small urban vegetable farms—*organopónicos*—were created in vacant lots in cities and towns across Cuba.

Bottom: Moíses Sío Wong explains operation of urban garden he initiated in Miramar district of Havana, the first to become a success. From right, Gustavo Chui, Cuban editor Iraida Aguirrechu, and Mary-Alice Waters.

Vegetables grown there supply three child-care centers and the Cesáreo Fernández elementary school, which serves lunch to 400 children daily. Thanks to such initiatives, "eating habits are beginning to change" as fresh vegetables become more a part of Cuban children's diet.

Top: Left, classroom in Cesáreo Fernández school. Right, schoolyard decorated with original art and sculpture by prominent Cuban artists.

This photo and below: Martín Koppel/Militant   Luis Madrid/Militant

Facing the food crisis

WATERS: The development of small-scale farming, in urban areas especially, has been one of the important initiatives Cuba has taken during the Special Period. The creation of these *organopónicos*, as they're called, in every municipality was a response to severe food shortages Cuba faced in the early 1990s. It has led to marked improvements in quantity and quality of fresh vegetables available for most Cubans. Today the organoponics involve the labor of almost as many Cubans as does traditional large-scale agriculture.

General Sío Wong, you are one of the people who has helped lead this effort from the beginning, so you're in a good position to tell us about it.

SÍO WONG: Let me start further back.

When the revolution triumphed in 1959, more than 80 percent of the arable land was held by large private estates owned by Cuban and by US ruling-class families like the Rockefellers, DuPonts, and Morgans, who had controlling interests in giant corporations such as United Fruit and the Cuban Electric Company. The US-owned Cuban-Atlantic Sugar Company, for example, owned more than 600,000 acres. The United Fruit Company owned almost 300,000. There were cattle ranches of tens of thousands of acres in Camagüey.

During the early years of the revolution, the agrarian reform—carried out in two stages, the first in 1959, the second in 1963—established that there would be no landholdings greater than five caballerías. A caballería, one of the units of measurement we use here in Cuba, is 13.4 hectares, so that would come to some 67 hectares, or 165 acres. Everything above five caballerías—that is, the giant holdings of the US ruling-class families and their corporations, as well as the big Cuban-owned plantations—was nationalized. Virtually all those landowners left the country, despite the fact they were offered compensation.[1]

As for the remaining land, the agrarian reform law turned it over to the peasants who had worked those parcels as sharecroppers, tenant farmers, squatters, or small sugarcane growers. Before the revolution these peasants mostly worked little plots of land, often paying rent in kind that could equal as much as half their produce. Nevertheless, the land didn't belong to them. So the revolution—their revolution—issued these peasants title to their land, up to 5 caballerías, about 165 acres. A hundred thousand deeds were given out.

Through the agrarian reform, some 20 percent of the arable land became holdings of small farmers, and 80 percent became state land. Our revolution had a policy of not dividing up the large estates, as occurred in other countries that had carried out an agrarian reform. That was a very wise decision Fidel and other leaders made, not to divide up the big holdings. State-owned sugar-producing enterprises and large cattle-raising enterprises were created on this 80 percent.

Early on we developed trade relations with the Soviet

1. Landowners were offered bonds, redeemable in twenty years, that paid 4.5 percent annual interest. The assessed value of their land was to be based on the value declared by the landowners themselves in October 1958 for tax purposes.

Union on favorable terms. When the price we had to pay the USSR for oil went up, so did the price at which we sold them sugar. On long-term contracts, which is how most sugar is sold on the world market, the Soviets would pay us up to 40 cents a pound, even if the market price had fallen to 10 or 15 cents. That was advantageous for us. The advantage for them was that producing beet sugar at home cost them up to 80 cents a pound.

We organized Cuba's whole agricultural production around those relations. We're often criticized for developing our agriculture that way. But it enabled us to build dams and reservoirs, bring electricity to the countryside, and create the whole agroindustrial infrastructure we now have.

By 1989, in fact, Cuba had more tractors per arable hectare of land than any other country in the world. Cuba has seven and a half million hectares of arable land, close to 20 million acres, and in 1989 we had 110,000 tractors. There were so many tractors, and fuel was so cheap, that people didn't use them just for farming but even for transportation. To take a drive. To go visit your girlfriend.

From that point of view, economic relations with the Soviet Union were favorable for a small country like ours. The USSR benefited too from the standpoint of long-term stable supplies of sugar and, to a lesser extent, other products.

WATERS: From the very first days, as Fidel stated in 1960, self-sufficiency in food and diversification of agriculture was the goal of the revolution. But that's not what happened. Cuba's minister of sugar, Ulises Rosales del Toro, reminded the National Assembly of this a few years ago, noting that that strategy had been postponed because of the "market at fair and stable prices with the USSR and other socialist countries" you've been describing.

What did this concentration on sugar production and trade

mean for the cultivation of food crops?

SÍO WONG: Cuba used to be an exporter of vegetables. There used to be a ferry from Havana to Key West. It took seven hours. My family lived by the Malecón, and I remember the steamship *Florida* coming in. I used to see trucks full of tomatoes, beans, and lettuce coming in to be loaded onto that ship.

But we came to be an importer of vegetables. In bottles and cans, the vegetables came from Bulgaria, Albania, the Soviet Union—in exchange for sugar.

Onset of Special Period

By the beginning of the 1990s, the Soviet Union and the socialist camp had fallen, and overnight the Special Period in Cuba began. The country was practically paralyzed. We had to adopt measures we had foreseen for times of war—in the event of a military blockade or aggression interrupting the flow of supplies. We referred to these measures, in their totality, as the "Special Period in Peacetime," since the same measures had been anticipated for a special period in wartime, facing the necessity to function without fuel imports and other resources.

We used to receive 13 million tons of oil annually, which we got from the Soviet Union in long-term trade agreements at special prices. It was bought with our sugar, as I described. Suddenly we had to begin working with 6 million tons of oil bought on the world market, at world market prices. Eighty-five percent of our trade had been with the Soviet Union and the other socialist countries. Suddenly, instead of being able to import $8 billion worth of goods, we had only $2 billion to buy a little oil, as well as essential food and medicines, on the world market. Our ability to purchase goods from abroad dropped by almost 80 percent.

All those gas-guzzling tractors stopped running. The buses

stopped running. The government of China began sending us millions of bicycles. Do you remember how Havana in the early 1990s started looking like Beijing, with millions of bicycles? Millions.

In 1993, in face of the economic crisis, the government took a whole series of measures in order to save the revolution. Many of them we didn't like, since they increased inequalities. We had always fought for a more just society, a socialist society, one that guarantees the basic needs of the whole population: health, education, food, housing, everything.

But we had no choice. One measure was allowing free circulation of the dollar. Previously it had been prohibited by law.[2] Agricultural markets were created, where farmers sold produce directly to the population at unregulated prices. Possibilities for self-employment were opened up. That's when the famous *paladares* arose—those little twelve-seat home restaurants, whose name *paladar* is taken from a Brazilian soap opera popular at the time. We began expanding international tourism. And we opened up avenues for foreign investment, along with the creation of mixed enterprises.

2. With the collapse of production in the early 1990s the value of the peso plunged. Officially pegged at 1 Cuban peso to the US dollar, by the summer of 1993 dollars traded for as much as 150 to 1 on the black market. In July 1993 circulation of the dollar was decriminalized, and stores were opened that sold imported goods for dollars. As the economic decline bottomed out during the Special Period and production recovered, the exchange rate stabilized at around 25 to 1.

    As part of its stepped-up economic pressure on Cuba, Washington increasingly blocked Cuba's use of dollars in international transactions. In response, in November 2004 the Cuban government announced that US dollars would no longer be allowed to circulate freely in Cuba. While Cubans are still able to receive US dollars, both they and tourists must exchange dollars for what are known as convertible pesos (CUC).

We had to stop providing lots of things free of charge. We began charging for sporting events like baseball, for instance, although not very much. How much does it cost now? One peso, two pesos? That's five or ten cents. Much less than in the United States, where a ticket to a baseball game can cost fifty or a hundred dollars.[3]

We don't like the inequalities that have arisen between those who have dollars and those who don't. That's why the so-called dollar stores were opened. They were established to bring in hard currency to pay for social programs that benefit everyone. Some of them even have the name TRD— Tiendas Recaudadoras de Divisas [Stores to Recover Hard Currency].

Creation of organoponic gardens

WATERS: What was the origin of urban small-scale vegetable farming?

SÍO WONG: I mentioned that one of the measures we took at the beginning of the Special Period was to expand tourism to bring in hard currency. But the expanding tourist hotels needed a growing supply of fresh vegetables. We had to fly these in from Mexico, Jamaica, and other countries. Our pilots began calling those trips "flights of shame." The tourism sector had to pay $35,000 for a single flight to bring in tomatoes and lettuce that, shamefully, were not being grown here.

On the wall here is a photo taken on December 27, 1987 [see photo section], a few years before the Special Period began. In it you can see Raúl Castro and Vilma Espín visiting a military unit. During that visit Raúl encountered an engineer named Ana Luisa Pérez, who had planted vegetables in some plan-

3.   In 2017, the average price for a ticket to a New York Yankees baseball game was $106.

tain pre-germinators with good results. He gave an order to develop and generalize this form of cultivation. A directive to that effect was issued to military units. Out of this came what we now call the *organopónicos*. The name comes from the fact that most of the inputs are organic.

General Néstor López Cuba was the first to start organoponic cultivation. The unit was one hectare in size. That's some two and a half acres. At the time he headed the 50th division, located in eastern Cuba. The organoponic farm there was built next to the base where the unit was headquartered and was worked by the families of officers and soldiers. López Cuba was an old campesino. He liked doing this.

An armed forces center was set up in Havana known as Hortifar, producing vegetables mainly.

So the organoponic gardens developed first within the armed forces. In the civilian sector we continued to import vegetables.

When the Fourth Party Congress was held in Santiago de Cuba in October 1991, the Special Period was just beginning. But it was already clear that our priority task was the food program. To produce food.

At the beginning of December, we held an assembly here at the National Institute of State Reserves and decided to create an organoponic garden. Fifty-four days later the first lettuce was harvested. We had already been clearing trash out of a vacant lot across the street, so we filled it with seed beds and planted. We started on December 5, 1991, and harvested the first lettuce on January 28, 1992—the anniversary of José Martí's birth.

Not everybody was happy with what we were doing, however.

I'll tell you a story. On December 31, 1991, at the military council within the Ministry of the Revolutionary Armed

Forces, I informed the minister [Raúl Castro] that we had begun building the garden and that many people were criticizing us: "How is it that in the Special Period you're using concrete blocks and cement, wasting such scarce materials, to build an organoponic vegetable garden?"

Raúl answered them. "I know that some leaders are criticizing Sío Wong," he said. "But what they should do is follow his example and produce food. Moreover, I'm the godfather of that organoponic farm."

Then Raúl asked me, "Well, how much are you going to produce?"

I'd heard that in China they produce 25 kilograms [55 pounds] of vegetables per square meter per year. So I told him, "I think we can get 25 kilograms per square meter."

A compañero took out a calculator: 25 kilograms per square meter equals 75,000 quintals per caballería [7.5 million pounds per 33 acres].

"Seventy-five thousand quintals per caballería! Are you crazy?"

If you get 10,000 quintals per caballería a year that's a lot—10,000 quintals of anything. Seventy-five thousand quintals would be extraordinary.

"Well," I said, "Let's try."

How did we start? First, we assigned two compañeros, the one in charge and the botanist. Then we created voluntary work brigades from the institute. For three years—1992, 1993, and 1994—we failed to go above 10 kilograms per square meter.

At the beginning of 1995 we requested permission to establish a new system of compensation, one that went against the established norms here in Cuba. Why did we do so? Farm work is one of the hardest jobs there is. This is true even of our conventional agriculture, which is mechanized with tractors, harvesters, and so on. Yet the average wage of a farm-worker is 148 pesos. The average wage in Cuba is about 250 pesos.[4] So we requested permission to provide an incentive. It's more like a cooperative, where the land is owned by the state, like the UBPCs created out of the state farms in 1993. Let me explain how the system works.

A worker at the *organopónico* gets an advance of 225 pesos a month—similar to an advance on wages—to cover expenses. The workers are charged for all the inputs: electricity, water, seeds, etc. Then 50 percent of the unit's net profit is divided among the workers. That's the first principle.

The second principle: the shares aren't equal. Profits are distributed under the rule that those who work more earn more.

The third principle: the person in charge earns 10 percent more than the highest-paid worker, as an incentive to take on overall administrative responsibility. One of the chief merits of this system is that those who work the land—who have some of the hardest jobs—deserve to be paid in accordance with output.

In other countries—as we're now seeing in Venezuela—it's the middlemen who make the most. The producer, the peasant producer, gets paid the least in capitalist countries. That's how it works in all these underdeveloped countries. And the same thing was happening here, even though we have state-owned distribution and marketing enterprises.

At the end of 1995 I reported to the Military Council that

4.   These figures correspond to wages prior to 2005. In April 2005 the minimum wage in Cuba was demonstratively raised from 100 to 225 pesos a month. Over 1.6 million workers, including the overwhelming majority of farmworkers, benefited from this measure, which raised the average wage in Cuba to 312 pesos a month. In 2016 the minimum wage in Cuba was 225 pesos, the average wage around 690.

we'd reached 30 kilograms per square meter—20 percent more than we had initially projected. "So what's responsible for the miracle?" they asked.

There is no "miracle," I said. The results are due to systematic, sustained, intensive work. For eight hours, nine hours, ten hours a day, out in the sun. Every day the plants have to be watered and tended. You have to come in on December 31, January 1, Christmas Day, May 1. There's no Saturday or Sunday off. Transplanting has to be done after 4:00 PM or else the sun will kill the plants. You have to weed, fertilize, thin the plants. You have to produce the organic material, everything.

But as a result, on that little piece of land you'll see 60 tons of vegetables produced per year. That's 30 kilograms per square meter of arable land, which comes to 300 tons per hectare. It's very intensive agriculture.

This is really when the movement to take advantage of all the free space in and around the cities began to take off.

We don't call it organic agriculture, because organic farming and organic products require international certification. There's an international agency that sets the standards. They come and measure the contamination levels and so on. But in fact we use virtually no chemical products. We use organic material and biological controls. That's why we say our farms are organoponic and agroecological. Our scientists work hard to find all the biological controls to fight pests. Because chemical pesticides, first of all, are very expensive and, secondly, can contaminate the environment. That's especially a concern here in the city. So we use organic materials and biological controls. We produce them in our laboratory here.

We use a localized irrigation system, invented by the Israelis, which is very efficient and uses a minimal amount of water. That too is an important strategic concern—to be able to grow food even if water supplies are disrupted, whether by drought or by enemy action. We also produce seeds for the entire country.

Growth of the movement

In 1995 there were only 257 hectares of organoponic agriculture in the whole country. To say it was OK for a worker to earn a thousand pesos a month was taboo. When Raúl Castro came here in 1997 after a trip we had taken to China, he looked out at the organoponic garden from my office on the fourth floor. It's not a crime to earn a thousand pesos a month through honest hard work—that was his conclusion. And he said so publicly.

After that, things began to change.

By 2003 we had 45,000 hectares of organoponic and intensive gardens. Look how production has increased—from 4,200 tons of vegetables in 1994 to almost 4 million in 2004.

We've now surpassed what I call conventional agriculture in output.

More than 380,000 people were working in small-scale urban agriculture at the end of 2004. About 420,000 work in conventional agriculture. Of the workers in urban agriculture, 82,000 are women. There are youth, mid-level technicians, almost 40,000 retirees, 10,000 professionals.

If you do the calculation, you'll see that up to twenty people can productively work each hectare (2.5 acres). Unemployment in Guantánamo was reduced from 7.1 percent in 2001 to 5.1 percent—in just two years. Santiago went from 9.1 percent to 2.9, Granma from 10.7 to 3.4. The greatest number of jobs created in recent years has been in agriculture—nearly 80,000 jobs. The overall unemployment rate by the end of 2003 was 2.3 percent. Internationally a rate less than 3 percent is considered very good.

The Special Period compelled us to develop this agricul-

ture, although it was a tremendous battle. The United Nations Food and Agricultural Organization (FAO) now recognizes that Cuba is the one country that has been able to
extend this small-scale agriculture on a mass scale. This is
something the people of the world want: to develop an ecological and sustainable agriculture that provides the food
the world's population needs, that protects the environment
and reduces pollution.

We've been able to develop that in Cuba because Cuban
workers and farmers made a socialist revolution. Agricultural production in Cuba is not driven by capitalist enterprises seeking to corner markets and maximize profits. It's
driven by the need to provide abundant food for health and
life.

Components of urban agriculture system

Agriculture production in Cuba is organized through several forms, and those engaged in urban agriculture are organized in several different ways. There are state enterprises.

There are Agricultural Production Cooperatives, the CPAs,
made up of farmers who have pooled their land. They own
and work it jointly.

There are Credit and Service Cooperatives, the CCSs, in
which farmers own and work their own land but help each
other and share services and equipment, receiving loans
from the government. They elect a leadership for the cooperative.

There are the UBPCs mentioned earlier, Basic Units of Cooperative Production. These were established in 1993 as former state farms were restructured and transformed into co-
ops. The land belongs to the state, but the product of labor on
the UBPCs belongs to the members of the cooperative who
work the land.

Then there are the backyards. People farm in their back-yards too.

And finally there are the *parceleros*: anyone who wants a parcel of land to work can get one.[5]

All these, to one degree or another, are engaged in urban agriculture, which is simply small-scale agriculture, nothing more. That's how it's known throughout the world.

We couldn't call it that at the beginning. Because our policy, in the Ministry of Agriculture and the leadership as a whole, was to develop large-scale agriculture, big enterprises. Small-scale agriculture was taboo. So we found another name: we called it urban agriculture.

But what is urban agriculture? Everything cultivated in the city of Havana and its surrounding area falls under that category. Everything within a ten-kilometer radius of the provincial capitals is designated urban agriculture. Everything within five kilometers of a municipality. Within two kilometers of each community with more than a thousand residents.

5.   In 2008 the Cuban government adopted Decree-Law 259, later expanded by Decree-Law 300, which provided for the free distribution of idle land to those who agreed to farm it. The measures were aimed at recovering land lost to production due to the scarcity of seeds, fertilizer, pesticides, and fuel during the Special Period. As of 2016, some 220,000 leases have been granted to working people in city and countryside, individual farmers, and farm cooperatives. Some 4.7 million acres have been distributed. Not all of this land is under cultivation, however, and an additional 2.2 million acres remain unclaimed.

In 2017 Decree-Law 300 was modified in several ways. Leases to individual famers were extended from ten years to twenty, and to cooperatives indefinitely. Permission was granted to build housing, storage, and other facilities on the land. And leaseholders were granted permission to establish contracts with agricultural cooperatives and state-run farms to increase their access to land-clearing equipment and other technical support.

That's all classified as urban agriculture. But it's nothing more than small-scale agriculture. The same thing is done in the city and its surroundings as in a small village. That's how small-scale agriculture was developed throughout the country. It's both urban and rural.

This agriculture doesn't just have the potential to increase the quantity of food available for consumption but also the quality. The United Nations Food and Agricultural Organization (FAO) recommends that adults consume between 300 and 400 grams of vegetables per day, no less than 300. It's what they recommend to get the vitamins and minerals the human body needs.

This is important, because the traditional Cuban diet consists of rice, beans, tubers, meat. Cubans ate very few vegetables. Maybe at Christmastime we ate tomatoes, lettuce, and radishes. But a culture of eating vegetables doesn't exist here. It's not like some other countries, like China, where it's a habit.

So in 2001 Fidel issued instructions that child-care centers and schools would get food provisions through the urban agriculture system. It was part of the Battle of Ideas and the improvement of education. This began here in Havana. Each organoponic garden, intensive orchard, or cooperative is linked to one or another school and also supplies child-care centers, old-age homes, hospitals, and so forth.

At our organoponic, INRE 1, for example, this practice had already begun in 1992. We provided vegetables to the day-care center a few blocks away. Now the enterprise supplies produce to three child-care centers, plus the Cesáreo Fernández elementary school, to which we're godparents and which we'll visit later today. Some 400 children eat lunch there each day, with a daily per capita of 125 grams of vegetables.

And we're making progress. Eating habits are beginning to change.

Take spinach. We began planting spinach. It used to be that Cubans didn't eat spinach. They called it Popeye food. Spinach has a lot of iron. Doctors began prescribing it for underweight children. So consumption is growing. People have gotten used to eating spinach, and now they ask for it. During the winter spinach grows a little slower, so that creates a problem.

The same with Swiss chard. People ask for it now. They eat it.

WATERS: How is distribution of food cultivated in the organoponic units organized?

SÍO WONG: It's sold directly to the population. The first principle: you sell it right where you produce it.

WATERS: There's no other distribution?

SÍO WONG: Yes, the Metropolitan Horticultural Enterprise, for example, has a warehouse. It buys produce and distributes it through state-run markets, sells it to hotels, to the tourist sector. It's a big enterprise with contracts with the farmers and also has its own *organopónicos*.[6]

We have what's called free agricultural markets, which are based on supply and demand.

But there are others, where prices are regulated. Like our prices are regulated here. Prices can't go above a maximum that's been set. These markets are called *topados*—meaning the prices have ceilings.

WATERS: Are the topados state-run?

6. In 2011, a new regulation allowed farm cooperatives and state-run farms to sell directly to hotels and restaurants. The measure was modified two years later to allow individual small farmers to do the same. The range of products that can be sold directly to tourist facilities has also increased.

síO WONG: Yes, a commission in the municipality meets monthly and fixes the prices. In the winter, for example, the price of lettuce goes down since production is high, but in the summer the price goes up. Each month there's a price list. There are some seventy capped markets here in Havana. Much of the production comes from the urban organoponic farms. And the Youth Army of Labor produces for the capped markets as well,[7] although their farms are in the countryside, not the city.

The place where prices are totally uncontrolled are the farmers markets, which I mentioned earlier. That is another type of market.

WATERS: Why would farmers sell in markets with price ceilings? Can't they earn more by selling in the unregulated markets? What's the incentive?

síO WONG: Many farmers benefit from the regulated markets because they don't have a way to transport their produce for sale at the unregulated markets. They have to pay a middleman. So they sign agreements to sell to the topados. The consumer benefits as well, since the prices are cheaper.

7. See glossary, Youth Army of Labor.

Capitalism, socialism, and the environment

WATERS: General Choy, you are currently president of the State Working Group to clean up Havana Bay. The Cuban government decided to take on this immense environmental challenge during the Special Period. Like the response to the food crisis that Sío Wong has described, it captures some of the ways in which the revolution has been strengthened. As Fidel put it, "someday we may have to erect a monument to the Special Period."

How did Havana Bay get into such bad shape, and how did the project to clean it up come about?

CHOY: Havana Bay and its port bear the main weight in Cuba's import and export trade. That's been true since colonial days. Some 70 percent of all imports enter by way of the port of Havana. And excluding sugar and nickel, 90 percent of the exports. The Ministry of the Sugar Industry has its own ports, and nickel is shipped from Moa.[8]

8. In 2014 the Cuban government opened a Special Development Zone at the Port of Mariel, 30 miles west of Havana. It includes a deepwater port, container terminal, and duty-free trade zone. The new facility, which can handle the largest container ships coming through the recently widened locks of the Panama Canal, is projected to replace Havana as the country's principal port. Container traffic has been increasingly shifted to Mariel, while

Prior to the revolution, as you would expect, the coastal ecosystem of the bay was not protected from indiscriminate contamination. During the early years of the revolution, the problem was recognized, but measures to clean up and preserve the bay weren't followed through.

It's not just the bay. The problem is also the hydrographic, or tributary, basin, which covers some seventy square kilometers. There are now 104 enterprises located in that zone that contaminate the bay.

Not to mention the sewage system, which is inadequate. Construction on the sewage system began in 1913 and finished in 1915. The city of Havana then had 300,000 inhabitants. The system was built for double that amount, for 600,000 people. But it now has to serve more than 800,000. There's insufficient drainage for all that water. So there's overflow in the streets.

Following the triumph of the revolution in 1959, various directives were issued and a few things were done. But there was no substantive progress. Commissions on the environment existed on the Havana provincial and municipal levels before the 1990s, and there were commissions on science, technology, and the environment in certain other areas—and still are. But an institution charged concretely with cleaning up the bay was not set up.

In 1996, 1997, and early 1998, as we were coming out of the worst years of the Special Period, the contamination problem was studied by Cuban research, scientific, and social institutions, with United Nations financing. The sources of the bay's dreadful environmental condition were determined. On June 15, 1998, the Executive Committee of the Council of Ministers

---

Havana continues to handle general cargo as well as cruise and other passenger ships.

voted to create the State Working Group for the Cleanup, Preservation, and Development of Havana Bay and its Tributary Basin. It's known by the initials GTE-BH (Grupo de Trabajo Estatal para el Saneamiento, Conservación, Desarrollo y Mantenimiento de la Bahía de La Habana y su Cuenca Tributaria).

The State Working Group leadership agreed to adopt the studies that had been done, as well as the twenty-one overall recommendations these studies had come to for cleaning up the bay. These recommendations became the basis of the group's work projections.

The first cleanup program was laid out over ten years, divided into two five-year periods. The year 2004 marked the completion of the first stage. The results are encouraging. Laboratory samples and tests of the water quality show a decrease in pollutants, and at the same time, the oxygen level has risen. This has enabled fish to begin returning to the bay, and following them, pelicans and gulls that feed on the fish.

Despite these small achievements, the waters continue to be in poor condition.

Intensive environmental and sanitation efforts are under way in collaboration with a number of national and international institutions, as well as some foreign governments, among them Belgium, Italy, Germany, and Japan.

Together with the Provincial Agricultural Delegation, reforestation of the bay's tributary basin has begun. Following the plan's completion in 2007, we will have planted more than a million saplings in order to purify and improve the capital's air quality and prevent fertile soil from being washed away with the runoff whenever there's heavy rain.

Together with the Provincial Directorate of Community Services, we are establishing a system to selectively recycle garbage first in the port area, and later throughout the entire basin.

Together with the Ministry of Public Health we're installing in the bay's outlet a system of seven atmospheric monitoring stations—the first of their kind in Latin America—that will automatically detect any negative variation in air quality and its origin. This will enable medical inspectors to locate the source of atmospheric contamination and demand that it be stopped.

We're building a large water treatment plant on the banks of the Luyanó River, one of the worst sources of contamination of the bay. It should be finished by the middle of 2006. This plant will be able to treat and purify up to 1,000 liters a second. In early 2005 construction began on another plant along the banks of the Luyanó. Its waters are very polluted because the river runs through San Miguel del Padrón, which has a larger number of factories than any other municipality in Cuba, and all the industrial waste goes into the Luyanó. Moreover, many people live along its banks, and the sewage water goes into the river.

The government's policy is to increasingly monitor the work done along the banks of the Luyanó, shifting production or moving enterprises that pollute the bay. For example, there were four slaughterhouses—three beef and one pork— that were relocated, because organic contamination from them was ending up in the river.

Related to the problem of the sewers, we received aid from the Japanese government to prepare a plan for draining rainwater runoff into Havana Bay and its tributary basin. Now we need to find the money to begin implementing the program in 2008. The plans call for the project to be completed in 2020.

KOPPEL: Does the Working Group have the power to enforce its decisions?

CHOY: Yes. We have jurisdiction over all questions concerning Havana Bay and its tributary basin. And we set demanding standards for everyone, including government ministries. Last week, for example, I sent a letter to the minister of basic industry. There had been a big spill at the Ñico López oil refinery, contaminating the bay and adversely affecting the state of the water. The minister of industry, who I sent the letter to, is a member of the Political Bureau. But we have a mandate from the government and we carry it out. No provincial or municipal commission has authority to do what we do.

In addition, if anyone plans to remodel any factory located on the bay or its tributary basin, or to build a new one, they have to submit the plans to us for approval. We analyze these projections, and then we inform the Ministry of Science, Technology, and the Environment (CITMA) whether we're in agreement. If we are, then CITMA gives the OK. If we don't give the go-ahead, they don't either.

This is a very complex effort. The entities contaminating the bay are responsible to eleven different ministries. These enterprises are spread out over ten of the fifteen municipalities in the capital. Each municipality has a vice president responsible for the environment, as well as a municipal environmental commission. In addition, there is a provincial environmental commission. In the area encompassing the bay and its tributary basin, there are forty-two people's councils. These are leadership bodies on the grassroots level.[9]

9. People's councils (*consejos populares*) were formed in neighborhoods, towns, villages, and rural areas of Cuba in 1992. They are local organs of People's Power, as Cuba's elected government bodies are called. The councils are composed, in their majority, of elected delegates, plus representatives designated by the mass organizations (trade unions, women's federation, etc.), the Communist Party and Union of Young Communists, and the principal institutions and enterprises in the area. The councils are charged

So we have to involve many people and many organizations in the work. It's a challenge, but we're achieving it.

Port of Havana

WATERS: You have another responsibility that's closely related, involving the operation of the Port of Havana.

CHOY: I'm the representative of the minister of transportation in the port of Havana, where I organize the port's administration. This is something new in Cuba.

A law on ports used to exist here. With various modifications, it went back to colonial days. In 2002 a new law on ports was adopted. It established a system of port administration, starting here in Havana. At that point I was named president of the administration of the Port of Havana. Like the State Working Group, it's something that never before existed in Cuba. We had to acquire experience as we went along.

Our work involves maritime operations at the port. We organize the arrival of ships, decide where they're going to dock, and supervise unloading, release of cargo, and shipping out.

WATERS: The port workers historically have been one of the most class-conscious and combative sectors of the working class in Cuba . . .

CHOY: Yes, very combative, very revolutionary.

WATERS: . . . and a large percentage of the port workers have always been black.

CHOY: Yes. In fact, in the ports, stevedores in Cuba were long referred to simply as the "blacks down below."

with maximizing efficiency in production and services in their areas, and promoting the greatest possible participation and local initiative by the population to solve problems. They facilitate cooperation between the existing entities in their area, and monitor programs they develop.

Capitalism is responsible for the destruction of the environment

[The developed capitalist societies are] the main ones responsible for the appalling destruction of the environment. . . .

It is not possible to blame this on the countries of the Third World, formerly colonies and now nations exploited and plundered by an unjust world economic order.

The solution cannot be to prevent the development of those who need it the most. . . .

Unequal trade, protectionism, and the foreign debt constitute ecological assaults and promote destruction of the environment.

To save humanity from this self-destruction, there must be a better distribution of the planet's available wealth and technology.

FIDEL CASTRO
RIO DE JANEIRO
JUNE 1992

Today stevedores earn a very good wage, in addition to a bonus in convertible currency. Sometimes, depending on the number of ships that come in, they earn 50 or 60 dollars a month, up to 100 dollars. That's on top of their normal monthly wage, which is between 220 and 350 pesos. The administrators and those who work in an office earn less. The stevedores earn the most—the ones down below, carrying sacks, unloading ships, loading trucks.

The port works 24 hours a day. The work shifts are 7 hours, 20 minutes. In exceptional cases, the stevedores may agree to work twelve-hour shifts, but those cases are rare.

In addition, special attention is given to meeting workers' needs on the job, a job that is difficult and strenuous. It's extremely hot, for example, down below, in the ship's storage holds where the stevedores work. So, cold water is constantly lowered down to them.

KOPPEL: What you're describing reflects a different social reality from that lived by workers under capitalism.

CHOY: That's the point I'm trying to make.

WATERS: Let's go back to the fact that the clean up of Havana Bay was undertaken as an urgent task right in the midst of the Special Period. That's striking.

CHOY: In the early 1990s, when Fidel publicly explained the measures we'd have to adopt in order for the revolution to survive, he said at the same time: "We're not only going to conquer the Special Period, we're going to continue developing." The creation of the State Working Group for the Cleanup, Preservation, and Development of Havana Bay is simply living proof that as we have conquered we've continued to develop.

WATERS: Throughout the capitalist world, especially in countries under the thumb of imperialist domination, environmental destruction is accelerating. Whenever it's a question of cleaning up or protecting the environment, capitalists argue it costs too much. Why is this different in Cuba?

CHOY: In 1992, at the Earth Summit in Rio de Janeiro, Brazil, our commander in chief, Fidel, stressed the urgent need for taking measures to restore and protect the environment and thereby save humanity.

Shortly after that, Cuba's National Assembly amended and broadened Article 27 of our constitution to spell out more explicitly the responsibilities of the Cuban state and people in relation to the restoration, preservation, and protection of the

'Cuban Revolution protects the well-being of future generations'

Amended Article 27 of the Cuban constitution, adopted in 1992, reads: "The State protects the environment and the country's natural resources. It recognizes their close connection with sustainable economic and social development to make human life more rational and assure the survival, well-being, and safety of current and future generations. The competent bodies will carry out this policy. It is the duty of citizens to help protect the water, the atmosphere, conserve the soil, vegetation, and all the rich potential of nature."

The previous version stated, "To assure the well-being of the citizens, the state and society protect nature. It is the responsibility of the competent bodies and also of each citizen to ensure that the waters and air are kept clean, and that the soil, vegetation, and animals are protected."

environment, and with it, of human civilization. We were the first country to do that after that summit.

This is possible because our system is socialist in character and commitment, and because the revolution's top leadership acts in the interests of the majority of humanity inhabiting planet earth—not on behalf of narrow individual interests, or even simply Cuba's national interests.

Cuba, Venezuela, and Latin America

WATERS: Sío Wong, you've spent a great deal of time recently in Venezuela, responding to a request to help develop the urban agriculture program there. Tens of thousands of Cubans are in Venezuela offering their services as doctors, nurses, technicians, teachers, sports instructors, and in other fields. How did this come about?

SÍO WONG: What's developing in Venezuela is a revolution, in my opinion, a Bolivarian revolution. The banners of liberty and Latin American integration, first unfurled by Simón Bolívar, are being raised by a people who are showing themselves capable of confronting imperialism, neoliberalism, and the national oligarchy. Hugo Chávez Frías, the president, is a leader who is charismatic, honest, patriotic, and Bolivarian.

Venezuela is an immensely rich country, with untapped wealth. Not just oil. It's a country of nearly a million square kilometers with immense land, water, and mineral resources. Fishing resources, water resources, lumber resources, mineral resources—including iron, bauxite, gold, and diamonds.

Yet Venezuela is a country in which 80 percent of the population lives in poverty, many in extreme poverty. You just have to go to the *cerros*, the poor neighborhoods in the hills, of Caracas to see how 80 percent of the population lives. And this is in a country that's among the top five oil exporters in the world. It's the third-largest supplier of oil to the United States. It's a country that has the capacity to produce 3 million barrels a day.

It's estimated that more than $700 billion in profits was generated by workers in the oil industry there between 1958 and 1998. Yet more than two million people were illiterate. Many had no access to medical care or education. What did all the supposedly democratic governments do in the forty years following the overthrow in 1958 of the Pérez Jiménez dictatorship? That $700 billion was stolen from the Venezuelan people. That's what those governments oversaw.

So the current government came in proposing what Chávez called a social revolution. The emphasis is on social projects.[10] For close to three years, the Chávez government was unable to carry out that perspective because the heart of Venezuela's economy is in the hands of the oil company, PDVSA [Petróleos de Venezuela, S.A.]. It's supposedly state-owned, yet the government did not have the resources available to move these social programs forward.[11]

This is not like the Cuban Revolution. The oligarchs and the rich didn't leave Venezuela because Chávez was elected. In the first couple of years after the Cuban Revolution triumphed in 1959, the workers and farmers carried out the

10. According to the United Nations' Economic Commission for Latin America and the Caribbean, social programs carried out by the Chávez administration helped reduce what ECLAC defined as the poverty rate from 49 percent to 28 percent of the population from 1999 to 2010.

11. The government of Venezuela nationalized oil in 1975. When the businesses owned by foreign companies and Venezuelan capitalists became state property, however, the operations of the new company—PDVSA—were left in the hands of the previous management.

agrarian reform, nationalized industry, and instituted other social measures. As that happened, all the rich, all the owners of plantations and companies, all the owners of mansions abandoned the country and went to Miami. That hasn't happened in Venezuela. They're still there. A large part of the economic power—the companies, the factories, the markets, the stores, transportation—all these remain in private hands. The wealthy have the power of the media in their hands. For these reasons, it's a very different situation.

First the imperialist-backed forces carried out a coup d'état that was beaten back. Then there was the oil coup, and most recently the recall referendum.[12] After defeating the attempted coups and winning the recall referendum by a landslide, the Bolivarian revolution, the popular forces, are stronger politically and economically.

PDVSA is now the source of the financial resources and in-

12. In an April 2002 attempted coup, Chávez and a number of his ministers and government officials were arrested. In response, hundreds of thousands of working people from the poor neighborhoods of Caracas poured into the streets. In face of this massive show of support for the Chávez government, the military divided and the coup collapsed after two days.

In December 2002 the US-backed capitalist forces opposed to Chávez began a "general strike," attempting to bring down the government. In reality this was a bosses' lockout, spearheaded by management at the state-owned oil company, and it initially paralyzed much of Venezuela's economy. Working people mobilized to restore production. Within two months the lockout, with dwindling popular approval, was defeated. The majority of the executives of PDVSA were fired for their role in organizing the action.

In 2004 the imperialist-backed opposition tried once again to oust Chávez, this time through a recall referendum that took place August 15. With a massive, organized effort by workers and farmers throughout the country, the referendum was defeated, with more than 59 percent voting "no."

frastructure to push forward social and economic programs, for example. Economic and political relations with countries of the Americas and the rest of the world have been broadened and consolidated. This has made Venezuela an important actor on the world stage, not just an exporter of oil. The main thing is the leadership it is providing on the difficult road toward Latin American and Caribbean integration, fulfilling the dreams of Bolívar and Martí.

The Bolivarian Alternative for the Americas (ALBA), launched by Chávez and Fidel in December 2004 in Havana, marks an important step in confronting US moves to exert greater dominance through the establishment of the Free Trade Area of the Americas (FTAA).

Cuba's collaboration

KOPPEL: When did Cuban internationalist aid begin?

SÍO WONG: Chávez received our support and collaboration from the time of his victory in the 1998 elections onward. But it wasn't until the December 1999 disaster in Vargas that Cuba, responding to requests for help, sent a medical brigade, composed of hundreds of doctors.[13] Working under very difficult conditions, this brigade brought solidarity and aid to the victims and to the population as a whole. The medical brigades did a magnificent job. Afterward we kept up the collaboration, in these fields and others, through agreements between the two countries.

One of the first programs was Barrio Adentro [Into the Barrio]. It began in 2003 in the hills surrounding Caracas and was later extended to the whole country. It's a project of

---

13. In December 1999 mudslides and flash floods battered Venezuela's Caribbean coast, leaving up to 50,000 people dead. The state of Vargas was the hardest hit.

medical collaboration, with Cuban doctors working in the poorest areas.

At the same time, President Chávez asked for collaboration in developing a literacy program. We've had experience in that field in Cuba. In 1961 we mobilized a hundred thousand young people and taught more than a million people to read and write, eradicating illiteracy in a single year. Later we developed materials for literacy programs in Portuguese, English, French, and Creole. We've had experience with programs in Haiti, in Africa, in many other places. So the Venezuelans asked for our help.

Our educators came up with a program utilizing videos that has revolutionized the speed at which students of all ages can learn. In Cuba the student-teachers lived with families for a year, including in the most isolated rural areas, and taught them using pencils, workbooks, and primers—the classic learning method. In Venezuela it's been possible to teach adults to read and write in seven weeks, with 64 half-hour lessons on video. This was done first in an experiment involving nearly 400 people, to see what the problems were. The results were that 87 percent of the students learned to read and write in seven weeks.

This program was extended to the mass level and named Mission Robinson.[14] Thousands of Venezuelan youth participated. The armed forces participated, providing needed logistical support to create fifty thousand classrooms throughout the country—each with a VCR, a television set, course materials, and facilitators.

14. Mission Robinson is named after Simón Rodríguez, who served as teacher to Simón Bolívar. Rodríguez's pseudonym was Robinson, which he chose because of his enthusiasm for the novel *Robinson Crusoe* by Daniel Defoe.

It was the Venezuelans themselves who did this. It's said that we sent thousands of Cuban teachers. But that's inaccurate. What we brought was our experience and the program. It was Venezuelan volunteer teachers who organized and led the classes. More than 1.5 million Venezuelans have now been taught to read and write. It won't be that long before the country can declare itself a Territory Free of Illiteracy.

But the education program didn't stop there. It continued with Mission Robinson II. This program is what we in Cuba called the Battle for the Sixth Grade. In Cuba it lasted close to ten years. Ten years, to organize for everyone in the country to reach the sixth grade. In Venezuela using audiovisual materials they're confident they will do it in much less. The classrooms for Mission Robinson II are already built.

Then there's Mission Ribas, which involves continuing on and obtaining a high school diploma. And Mission Sucre, which involves close to 400,000 high school graduates who formerly had no access to the university.[15] These graduates have been given scholarships to study and work, as well as a $100 monthly stipend. And with that they're able to enroll at the university. The government took a number of administrative buildings that had previously belonged to PDVSA and created the Bolivarian University in Caracas.

That's the educational program.

As for medical assistance, after Barrio Adentro got started, Chávez said that anyone who wants Cuban doctors in their neighborhood should just say the word. Because the opposition was trying to block the Barrio Adentro program in states

15. These programs were named after José Félix Ribas (1775–1815) and Antonio José de Sucre (1795–1830). Both were leaders of the fight for Venezuelan independence and for the independence of Latin America as a whole.

and municipalities they controlled.

Within four or five months, Cuba sent 10,000 doctors to Venezuela. These doctors are working in the poorest neighborhoods. Through the Family Doctor system, more than 17 million Venezuelans now have access to treatment.[16]

Venezuela is redesigning its medical system, beginning with primary care, then clinics, then hospitals. There are also private clinics and hospitals, of course, but the big majority of working people have little or no access to them. The public health system is being rebuilt based around preventive medicine. With care provided by a doctor who is right there in the neighborhood. Each one serves 120 families.

Six hundred diagnostic centers have been created, including thirty-five high-technology ones, with rooms for intensive therapy, dentistry, ophthalmology, rehabilitation, and clinical laboratories with state-of-the-art equipment.

In addition to the doctors, there are several thousand Cuban dentists. Other services are being set up as well, such as eye care. One of the difficulties Mission Robinson ran into was that many people who had trouble learning to read and write couldn't see well. So 300,000 pairs of glasses were sent, including progressive lenses, as well as vision-testing equipment. Thousands of patients with various diseases have come to Cuba for medical care. And there is a special program for cataract and other eye diseases, called Operation Miracle.

Thousands of sports instructors are part of the Barrio Adentro plan, too. They're organizing physical education and recreation programs in the communities. They've organized popular sports, children's sports, and gyms for the elderly.

As part of Cuba's collaboration, there's also the program

16. As of 2016 there were nearly 29,000 doctors, nurses, and other Cuban medical personnel serving in Venezuela.

I'm involved in, developing intensive vegetable cultivation, that is, small-scale urban agriculture. Not just in Caracas but throughout the country.

Urban agriculture program

KOPPEL: How did it begin?

SÍO WONG: In 2000 the general director of the United Nations Food and Agriculture Organization (FAO) based in Rome, Mr. Jacques Diouf, who is from Senegal, was here in Havana. He toured our center, and I explained to him our program for developing organoponic agriculture.

In February 2003 Mr. Diouf went to Venezuela. A food security program exists between the FAO and Venezuela.[17] The oil company's attempted coup against Chávez had just been defeated, but there was a food crisis, since the owners of the big food warehouses had joined in the economic sabotage.

Diouf told the Venezuelan government that the fastest way to produce food was urban agriculture. Cuba was the country with the most experience in that, he said. Diouf suggested that since Chávez is a friend of Fidel Castro, he should call Fidel and ask him to send General Sío Wong to help.

Within 48 hours I was on a plane to Venezuela, together with Adolfo Rodríguez Nodals, the director of INIFAT [National Institute of Basic Research in Tropical Agriculture] as well as the National Urban Agriculture Group. Also assigned to the mission were Dr. Miriam Carrión Ramírez and Miguel Salcines, an engineer.

Through an FAO project they've begun to develop organo-

---

17. The UN Food and Agriculture Organization has a Special Program for Food Security, which "aims to help those living in developing countries ... improve their food security through rapid increases in food production and productivity."

ponic agriculture in Venezuela. The initial idea was for us to be there for ten or twelve days to orient the specialists and then return to Venezuela every two or three months to check how the work is going. It actually was the other way around. We spent two or three months there and then I came back to Cuba for two or three weeks to work here.

We arrived February 20, 2003. On February 25 we met with President Chávez to present our experiences. On March 15 the president inaugurated the Fuerte Tiuna organoponic farm, and on March 28 the Bolívar 1 farm in downtown Caracas.

Bolívar 1 is right in the middle of the city, near the two towers and the Caracas Hilton. The Venezuelans provided a patch, sort of like a park, that was previously full of garbage. As we were designing it, we tried to fit in with the surroundings. "We can't cut down those palm trees," I said. Then it occurred to us that we should make it like the nearby Plaza Venezuela, which is circular in design. So we built a water tank in the middle, with a fountain over it, and the beds are circular. It's really quite artistic.

This is an arduous job, because we face the same difficulties and widespread lack of understanding about organoponic cultivation that we faced here in Cuba.

But urban agriculture can more and more serve as a source of employment, in addition to becoming a source of food in Venezuela.

Defending Venezuela, defending Cuba

WATERS: The US-backed opposition is carrying out quite a campaign against the assistance Cuba is giving.

SÍO WONG: A big slander campaign has been waged by the opposition to the Chávez government, targeting Cuban doctors above all. Cuban doctors, they claim, aren't qualified physicians. They're taking jobs away from Venezuelan doctors. The opposition has tried, without success, to accuse the Chávez government of using these doctors to "Cubanize" Venezuelan society.[18] A similar campaign is being waged in the United States, of course.

The four commercial television stations in Caracas all belong to the opposition. The government has one TV station, with the oldest and most obsolete equipment. Practically all the newspapers and radio stations in Venezuela belong to the opposition, as well. But its propaganda crusade has failed.

The opposition has tried to attack the quality of the care Cuban doctors are providing. They even alleged that a child died due to poor treatment. But a substantial layer within the population itself is taking responsibility to win broad acceptance for the program. Because not only does Barrio Adentro offer 24-hour-a-day medical care, but 105 different medications are being distributed free of charge. Insulin for diabetics, for one.

According to a recent study, these volunteer doctors are seeing 1.5 million patients a month and have saved an estimated 7,000 lives. What's considered a life saved? It's when the person would have died had medical treatment not been applied in time. Either because the person didn't get to the doctor in time, or due to lack of money.

In 2003 CNN made a big ruckus about some Cuban doctors defecting. There were 10,000 Cuban doctors in Venezuela then. Three or four took off. What percentage is that? If US

18. In June 2003 the Venezuelan Medical Federation (FMV) filed suit asking the courts to bar Cuban doctors from practicing. A lower court decision granting the request was overturned by higher courts. In July 2005 several hundred FMV members held a protest in downtown Caracas claiming Cuban volunteers are taking the jobs of Venezuelan doctors.

doors were suddenly flung open and every Venezuelan, Colombian, and Mexican who wanted a visa were granted one, how many do you think would go? Because many people in Latin America want to go to the US in hopes of having a better life, from an economic point of view.[19]

The medical and literacy programs, Barrio Adentro and Mission Robinson, have had a tremendous social impact.

I lived in Venezuela for almost a year, and I was able to observe the change. When we were building the first organoponic in the downtown park there, I asked some workers, "How come you're not with Chávez? If the previous governments haven't done anything for you in forty years, why aren't you supporting Chávez?"

The response back then was: "I don't support him because for three years Chávez hasn't given me a thing. I'm still poor."

But a transformation in popular opinion is under way. All these social and economic programs have created a shift. That's the reality.

When I arrived in Venezuela, I was one of the first Cubans who climbed the *cerros* of Caracas. Rather, I should say that I was one of the first *Fidel Castro* Cubans, since there are

---

19. In 2006 the US government started what is called the "Cuban Medical Professional Parole Program" designed to undercut the effectiveness of Cuba's medical assistance programs in dozens of countries around the world. The program offered refugee status and permanent US residence to any Cuban medical professional serving abroad who applied for it by walking into a US consulate anywhere in the world. Over the following decade, the US government claimed to have approved more than 7,000 such applications. Washington ended the program in January 2017 along with the so-called "wet foot/dry foot" policy, which guaranteed US permanent residency to any Cuban who set foot on US soil.

Since the beginning of the revolution, more than 325,000 healthcare volunteers have served in 158 countries.

other kinds of Cubans there. I spent several days wandering through those neighborhoods to determine where to build an organoponic farm. As in many Latin American cities, the *cerros* are the poor areas, where no one else ever ventures. In Rio de Janeiro, for instance, no one who doesn't live in the favelas ever goes there. Not even the police—or when they do, it's with guns blazing.

But in Venezuela we coordinate plans with the people from those communities, and they themselves organize security. The Cuban doctors are more protected and secure than almost anyone, because the residents themselves look after them.

I remember a recent program on Venezolana de Televisión—the state channel—interviewing a resident of one of those communities. "Look, I'm not a Chavista," the man said, when he learned the crew was from Venezuelan Television. "But if anyone lays a finger on the Cuban doctor, he's going to have me to answer to. Because she saved my son's life." That's typical of the popular reaction.[20]

This is our modest contribution to the Bolivarian revolution. It shows the internationalist spirit we've been educated in. Earlier we said we were trained in that spirit because we're paying a debt to history. A debt to those Africans, to those Chinese, to those from the Dominican Republic, from Venezuela, from the United States, from Poland, all of whom fought in Cuba's wars of independence. So we have that duty. Our doctors and other volunteers go to Venezuela with the same spirit our internationalists went to Angola,

---

20. There have been a handful of incidents of physical attacks on Cuban internationalist doctors. A doctor was killed in Araguá state in 2003, and a Venezuelan assistant to a Cuban medical volunteer was killed in Caracas in 2004.

Ethiopia, and Nicaragua with.

The other day Chávez spoke about how he'd met with some Cuban doctors and then decided to send them some mattresses, some beds. Because he'd been informed that some of them were sleeping on the floor.

So a Cuban went up to him and said, "Mr. President, we want to live as they live." And he wouldn't accept the mattresses.

"That doctor taught me a lesson," Chávez said.

WATERS: The Cuban doctors and other volunteers are also learning many lessons about the realities of capitalist society.

SÍO WONG: Yes, they are. The three of us—Chui, Choy, and myself—lived under capitalism. We know what it is. But young people here born since 1959 don't know. Now they're living it. Now they're seeing people who lack money to pay for medicine, who lack money to pay for school, who lack money to pay for food. They see people without a job. That's the reality they see. And they ask themselves how this could happen in a country that produces three million barrels of oil a day.

The imperialists say we're subverting Latin America. They call us subversives. But the objective conditions in Latin America offer no way out. Argentina is an example. Bolivia is an example. Peru is an example. Ecuador is an example. Brazil. What can the imperialist system offer? What can capitalism, the neoliberal model or any other variant, give them? It has resoundingly failed throughout Latin America.

Millions live in the *cerros* of Caracas, and the people poured down from them to defend Chávez against the coup. The imperialists are afraid of those *cerros*.

When I was climbing those hills, people would come up and say, "We're all Chavistas here."

"I'm with Chávez too," I replied. "Fidel, Raúl, and Che made me climb a lot of hills. Now, in my late sixties, I'm still climbing hills. For Venezuela."

Perhaps they thought I was a Japanese journalist when they saw me with a camera.

No, I responded. "I'm a Cuban. I'm one of Fidel's Cubans."

The Battle of Ideas

KOPPEL: You've referred to what is known in Cuba today as the Battle of Ideas. Can you explain what this is?

SÍO WONG: Defenders of capitalism seek to impose their culture, their ideas, on everyone. They strip peoples all over the world of our own cultures. The imperialists possess supremacy in technology and science. Some they've developed, some they've stolen. They dominate the media and information systems worldwide, through which they attempt to impose their values and justify their social relations.

This is why the Battle of Ideas is so important and so complex. Our ability to wage this battle rests largely on education, on teaching, on culture. On the example we provide children and young people.

We're now beginning another revolution, this one in the education of our children. "One must be educated to be free," as Martí put it. How can our children, our young people, and consequently our men and women be truly free if they aren't educated to think for themselves? How can they contribute to the development of the country? The era when many thought there was a textbook, a blueprint, for building socialism, is no more. We have to adjust our course to our reality, and to the reality of the world today.

Before the revolution 95 percent of us here in Cuba, maybe

more, considered ourselves anticommunists, even though we didn't know what socialism was. We were taught by comic books like Superman and Tarzan and Blackhawk. Blackhawk was one of our favorites. It was about a squadron of fighter pilots, and the characters included a Swede, a Frenchman, a Chinaman, a Pole. Communists were made out to be really bloodthirsty. The Chinese character, a cook named Chop-Chop, was a racist caricature. That's the type of thing they taught us, even at school. We lived that on a daily basis.

There's a famous story from the early years of the revolution about a meeting Fidel held with some peasants and workers.

"Do you agree with the urban reform?" Fidel asked them.

"Yes."

"Do you agree with the agrarian reform?"

"Yes."

"Do you agree with the nationalization of industry?"

"Yes."

"Do you agree with socialism?"

"Oh no, we don't agree with socialism!"

That's the way it used to be.

So what moment did Fidel choose to proclaim the socialist character of the revolution? He chose the opening of imperialism's attack on us at the Bay of Pigs in April 1961. It was then, as we buried our dead following the bombing of our airfields on April 15, that Fidel explained for the first time that our revolution is a socialist revolution. That air assault was the prelude to the mercenary invasion two days later.

As you know, most of the movies shown here in Cuba are made in the United States. We're not shut in. We don't live encased in a shell. People have access to the internet, and they have relatives in the United States. There's been a broad development of tourism. The key thing is to teach ourselves to think.

Since the triumph of the revolution we've been educated in socialism. We've been educated in selflessness: to be capable even of giving our lives for another people. That's the highest expression of human selflessness.

I went to Angola to risk my life for the Angolan people's struggle. What material benefit was there in that? None. And that's how tens and tens of thousands went—teachers, doctors, specialists. They went through many difficulties, and in the most remote places. How is this possible without consciousness?

But by the late 1990s there were 76,000 young people in Cuba who weren't going to school or working. As Fidel said, we had been remiss. The majority of these young people had family problems with divorced mothers and fathers, and so on. We had started categorizing them as "predelinquents." This terminology was horrendous! How was it possible? They were born within the revolution. They are products of the revolution. They are our children. Their parents were the generation that had gone to Angola, to Nicaragua, and had given their lives for the revolution.

The truth is, there had been shortcomings in our educational work. There had been shortcomings in our political work. In our social work. We recognize this. I believe this is Fidel's genius—to recognize shortcomings and to take measures to correct them. And not lose a minute in the process.

With the opening of the Battle of Ideas, all these young people were encouraged to study, and they received a stipend while doing so. The vast majority now believe they have a socially useful future.

This, I believe, is a cultural revolution. I don't like to use that phrase, since it brings to mind the Cultural Revolution in China. So let's call it an educational revolution. But that's what this great Battle of Ideas is: nothing other than a revolution within the revolution, so our entire people can get an integral and general education and culture.

I was explaining earlier that we have inequalities here that we don't like. More than 60 percent of the people here, for example, have access to hard currency. That means nearly 40 percent don't. I don't. But there are many people who do. They receive dollars or other convertible currency from their relatives abroad. Or they work someplace—such as in tourism, or in the tobacco, nickel, or electrical industries—that pays part of their wages in hard currency.

People often don't understand why prices are high at the dollar stores. I have to explain this to many people, including to businessmen who come here. These prices are set by the government to bring in hard currency, so we can pay for programs to compensate somewhat those who don't receive dollars. That's why prices in these stores are high.

We subsidize a number of items that everyone in Cuba has equal access to. Everyone receives medicine free of charge. Anyone here can have heart surgery without somebody asking about their bank account. Everyone receives education free of charge. Our social security system not only provides retirement income for every single citizen but also covers disability, maternity, and pregnancy leave. Some friends criticize us for maintaining these programs. But we're demonstrating how much can be done with very limited economic resources. The key thing is the human resources.

This battle we're engaged in is undoubtedly complex, but it's vital. You have to see how our children, our young people express themselves, their political level. We want to spread that as widely as possible, to make culture and education mass activities, to defend our national identity, our socialist identity. Above all, we want to teach young people to think.

CHUI: One organization that has occupied a vanguard position in the Battle of Ideas is the Association of Combatants of the Cuban Revolution. This is an organization of those who have fought to advance the Cuban Revolution and its internationalist missions. Compañeros who were in the Rebel Army, the clandestine struggle, fought at Girón, in the struggle against the counterrevolutionary bandits, or carried out an internationalist mission, whether as a combatant or as a doctor or teacher.

All the combatants are assigned schools and workplaces, where we give talks and lead discussions with the students, workers, and the community. We discuss our experiences in the revolutionary struggle and on internationalist missions. We disseminate the history of the revolution and its contributions elsewhere.

But it's not primarily about the past. Our history is still being written. We continue fighting every single day for the unconditional defense of our socialist revolution.

That's why the Association of Combatants is in the front ranks of the struggle for the freedom of our Five Heroes, fighters against terrorism unjustly held hostage in the prisons of the United States. Just as we're on the front lines in denouncing the aggressive policies of the US government toward our country.

CHOY: You've already heard our stories. You could write a book about Chui, about where he lived, where he worked. About how his father supported his family. The same with Moisés and how he was exploited by his brother-in-law.

Earlier I told you about the man who came into my father's store unable to feed his family because he didn't have seven cents. You heard about my friend who couldn't get into a dance because he was the son of a Chinese parent.

We know these things. We lived them. We suffered them. Nowadays young people don't see such things. They don't live that kind of discrimination because of skin color, economic means, or anything else. We may not have the healthiest diet, but everyone in Cuba has breakfast, lunch, and dinner. All children and young people up to the ninth grade are guaranteed lunch at school. Before the revolution not everyone was assured even of being able to go to school. Much less get health care.

We have to educate the youth to know about these things. We have to educate them so they know Cuba's history, so they know about the independence war against Spain, the war against the Batista dictatorship, the glorious victory at Playa Girón, the struggle against the counterrevolutionary bands, the internationalist missions. So they really understand what a revolution is, what socialism is.

These young doctors, teachers, sports trainers, and others who go abroad on internationalist missions—they're getting an education about the type of social system these countries have. They're seeing that our system is very different. They are learning that yes, a better world is possible. But only with a socialist revolution.

Glossary of individuals, organizations, and events

Abreu, Gerardo (Fontán) (1932–1958) – A young printshop worker, became a leader of Orthodox Youth, then head of July 26 Movement Youth Brigades in Havana from 1956. A leader of urban underground during revolutionary war. Captured, tortured, and murdered by dictatorship February 1958.

Acevedo, Enrique (1942–) – Joined Rebel Army July 1957 at age 14. Fought in Che Guevara's Column 8. Served in Angola 1977 and 1987–88, commanding tank brigade. Brigadier general (retired) in Cuba's armed forces.

Agramonte, Ignacio (1841–1873) – Major general in Liberation Army, based in Camagüey province, during Cuba's first independence war against Spain. Killed in battle.

Aldana, Carlos (1942–) – Joined July 26 Movement at age 14. Served in Rebel Army. Member of Communist Party Central Committee 1980–92, serving on Political Bureau and Secretariat. Headed Cuba's negotiating team during final stages of talks with Pretoria and Washington in 1988 to end Angola war. Sanctioned and removed from his responsibilities 1992.

Almeida, Juan (1927–2009) – Bricklayer and Orthodox Party member in Havana at time of 1952 Batista coup. Participated in 1953 Moncada attack; sentenced to ten years in prison. Released May 1955 following amnesty campaign. *Granma* expeditionary 1956. Promoted to commander February 1958.

Headed Third Eastern Front. After 1959 responsibilities included head of air force, vice minister of Revolutionary Armed Forces, and vice president of Council of State. One of three Sierra combatants to hold rank of Commander of the Revolution. A member of Communist Party Central Committee and Political Bureau 1965–2009. Hero of the Republic of Cuba. President of Association of Combatants of the Cuban Revolution from its foundation in 1993 until his death in 2009.

April 9 general strike – On April 9, 1958, the July 26 Movement called a general strike across Cuba in attempt to topple the dictatorship. Announced without adequate preparation, the action failed. Batista's forces responded with stepped-up repression and a major offensive against Rebel Army positions in the Sierra Maestra.

Association of Combatants of the Cuban Revolution (ACRC) – Founded 1993 as organization of combatants of Rebel Army, the urban clandestine struggle, Playa Girón, the struggle against counterrevolutionary bands, and Cuba's internationalist missions, both military and civilian. Its 300,000 members transmit the history and lessons of the revolution to new generations.

Authentic Party (Cuban Revolutionary Party) – Formed in 1934. Popularly known as *auténticos*, claiming to be authentic followers of José Martí's Cuban Revolutionary Party. Headed government 1944–52 under presidents Ramón Grau and Carlos Prío. Key component of bourgeois opposition to Batista 1952–58. Organized armed wing known as Authentic Organization. After fall of Batista regime, as revolution deepened during 1959–60, principal *auténtico* leaders left Cuba for US, where they joined counterrevolutionary forces.

Barredo, Lázaro (1948–) – Journalist and writer. Editor of Cuban daily *Granma* 2005–13; reporter for *Bohemia* magazine. Served as vice president of Union of Cuban Journalists and vice president of International Relations Commission of Cuba's National Assembly.

Batista, Fulgencio (1901–1973) – Military strongman in Cuba 1934–58. Led 1952 coup establishing dictatorship backed by Washington. Fled Cuba January 1, 1959, in face of advancing Rebel Army, popular insurrection, and general strike.

Bay of Pigs. *See* Playa Girón

Bolívar, Simón (1783–1830) – Latin American patriot, born in Caracas. Led series of armed rebellions 1810–24 that helped win independence from Spain for much of South America.

Bordón, Víctor (1930–2014) – Member of Orthodox Youth and later July 26 Movement in Las Villas. Formed July 26 Movement guerrilla unit operating in Escambray mountains that in October 1958 was integrated into Las Villas front led by Che Guevara. Attained rank of commander. Subsequently held national leadership responsibilities in Ministry of Construction, served as director of state metal manufacturing company Cometal.

Bu, José – Chinese-born officer in Cuban independence army, serving at side of General Máximo Gómez. Fought in Cuba's 1868–98 wars of independence, reaching rank of lieutenant colonel.

Cabral, Amilcar (1924–1973) – Founder and central leader of African Party for the Independence of Guinea-Bissau and Cape Verde (PAIGC), 1956. From 1963 led guerrilla war that won Guinea-Bissau's independence from Portugal in 1974 and Cape Verde's in 1975. Assassinated January 1973 by factional opponents in PAIGC urged on by Portuguese secret police.

Carreras, Jesús (1933–1961) – A leader of Second National Front of the Escambray. Joined armed counterrevolutionary bands in Escambray mountains after revolution's victory. Captured, tried, and executed.

Carrión Ramírez, Miriam (1945–) – Agricultural researcher at

INIFAT (Institute of Basic Research on Tropical Agriculture). Helped initiate small-scale agriculture project in Venezuela.

Castillo, Bárbara (1946–) – Minister of domestic trade 1995–2006. Member, Central Committee of Communist Party 1991–2011.

Castro, Fidel (1926–2016) – Student leader at University of Havana from 1945. A central organizer of Orthodox Party youth after party's founding in 1947. Orthodox Party candidate for House of Representatives in 1952 elections canceled by Batista following March 10 coup. Led revolutionary movement against Batista dictatorship that carried out July 26, 1953, attack on Moncada garrison in Santiago de Cuba and Carlos Manuel de Céspedes garrison in Bayamo. Captured, tried, and sentenced to fifteen years in prison. His courtroom speech, *History Will Absolve Me*, was distributed in tens of thousands of copies across Cuba, becoming program of revolutionary movement. Released in 1955 after national amnesty campaign, he led founding of July 26 Revolutionary Movement. Organized *Granma* expedition from Mexico, late 1956, and commanded Rebel Army during revolutionary war. Following revolution's triumph, was Cuba's prime minister from February 1959 to 1976. President of Council of State and Council of Ministers 1976–2008. Commander in chief of Revolutionary Armed Forces 1959–2008 and, Communist Party of Cuba's first secretary 1965–2011.

Castro, Raúl (1931–) – An organizer of student protests at University of Havana against Batista dictatorship, he participated in 1953 Moncada attack. Captured and sentenced to thirteen years in prison. Released May 1955 following national amnesty campaign. A founding member of July 26 Movement and a participant in 1956 *Granma* expedition. Promoted to commander in Rebel Army February 1958 and headed Second Eastern Front. Minister of the Revolutionary Armed

Forces 1959–2008. Vice premier 1959–1976. First vice president of Council of State and Council of Ministers 1976–2008; president since 2008. Second secretary of Communist Party of Cuba 1965–2011; first secretary since 2011.

Chávez, Hugo (1954–2013) – A lieutenant colonel in Venezuelan army, he headed failed 1992 military coup against government of Carlos Andrés Pérez and was imprisoned for two years. Elected president of Venezuela, 1998, 2000, 2006, and 2012. Together with Cuban president Fidel Castro, founded Bolivarian Alliance for the Peoples of the Americas (ALBA) in 2004. Used oil revenue to finance social programs in Venezuela and provide fuel at preferential prices to Caribbean nations. Workers, peasants, and youth have repeatedly mobilized to block attempts by Venezuelan bourgeoisie, with backing from Washington, to overthrow his government and that of his successor, Nicolás Maduro.

Chiang Kai-shek (1887–1975) – Leader of Kuomintang (Nationalist) Party in China from 1925. Led massacre of workers that brought bloody end to second Chinese revolution 1925–27. From 1927 headed dictatorship, overthrown by 1949 Chinese Revolution. Subsequently dictator of US-backed regime on Taiwan.

Chibás, Eduardo (1907–1951) – A leader of Student Directorate in fight against Machado dictatorship in 1920s and 1930s. Member of Authentic Party. In 1947 founding leader of opposition Orthodox Party (Cuban People's Party), which had broad popular support. Elected senator 1950. On August 5, 1951, in act of protest against government corruption, shot himself at close of radio address; died several days later.

Chomón, Faure (1929–) – Leader of Revolutionary Directorate and survivor of March 13, 1957, attack on Presidential Palace. Organized February 1958 expedition that established guerrilla front in Escambray mountains. Led integration of column into Las Villas front commanded by Che Guevara in October 1958. Attained rank of commander. Member of Communist Party Central Committee since 1965. A deputy in National Assembly of People's Power since 1976.

Cienfuegos, Camilo (1932–1959) – *Granma* expeditionary, 1956. Captain in Rebel Army Column 4 led by Che Guevara, promoted to commander 1958. From August to October 1958 led "Antonio Maceo" Column 2 westward from Sierra Maestra en route to Pinar del Río. Operated in northern Las Villas until end of war. Became Rebel Army chief of staff January 1959. Killed when plane lost at sea while en route from Camagüey to Havana, October 28, 1959.

Cintra Frías, Leopoldo ("Polo") (1941–) – From peasant family near Yara in eastern Cuba. Joined Rebel Army November 1957, finished war as a lieutenant. Commanded forces on Angola's Southern Front 1975–76. Internationalist mission in Ethiopia 1978. Headed Cuba's military mission in Angola 1983–86 and 1989. As commander of Southern Front from December 1987, led troops that defeated South African forces at Cuito Cuanavale and drove south to Namibian border in 1988. A Hero of the Republic of Cuba. Member of Communist Party Political Bureau since 1991. Minister of Revolutionary Armed Forces since 2011. Holds rank of army corps general.

Colomé Ibarra, Abelardo (1939–) – Joined Rebel Army March 1957 as member of Rebel Army's first reinforcement unit, reaching rank of commander. In 1962–64 served as internationalist volunteer in Argentina and Bolivia operating in support of guerrilla front in Argentina led by Jorge Ricardo Masetti. Headed Cuba's military mission in Angola 1975–76. Member of Communist Party Central Committee 1975–2016 and Political Bureau 1986–2016. Vice president of Council of State 1993–2013. Interior minister 1989–2015. Holds rank of army corps general (retired).

Cuban Five – Gerardo Hernández, Ramón Labañino, Antonio Guerrero, Fernando González, and René González, internationally known as the Cuban Five. Arrested 1998 in Florida, where they had been monitoring activities of Cuban counterrevolutionary organizations planning attacks on Cuban and US targets. Railroaded to prison by Clinton administration on fabricated charges including conspiracy to commit espionage and, in case of Hernández, murder. Three originally given life sentences. René González and Fernando González served entire sentences and released after more than fourteen and more than fifteen years, respectively. Guerrero, Labañino, and Hernández returned home December 17, 2014, when US-Cuba diplomatic relations were reestablished. Three of the Five—Hernández, Fernando González, and René González—served in Angola.

Cuban independence wars – From 1868 to 1898 Cubans waged three wars for independence from Spain. The Ten Years War of 1868–78, the "Little War" of 1879–80, and the war of 1895–98, leading to end of Spanish rule. US government occupied Cuba after Spain's defeat.

Cuban "Missile" Crisis (October Crisis) – In face of Washington's escalating preparations in spring and summer of 1962 to invade Cuba, Cuban government signed mutual defense agreement with the Soviet Union. In October 1962 US president John Kennedy demanded removal of Soviet nuclear missiles installed in Cuba following signing of pact. Washington imposed naval blockade of Cuba, stepped up preparations to invade, and placed armed forces on nuclear alert. Millions of workers and farmers mobilized to defend revolution. Following exchange of communications between Washington and Moscow, on October 28 Soviet premier Nikita Khrushchev, without consulting Cuban government, announced decision to remove the missiles.

Cuevas, Andrés (1915–1958) – Worker from village of Cama-
juaní in Las Villas. Joined Rebel Army early 1957, becoming
captain. Killed at Battle of El Jigüe, July 19, 1958. Posthumously
promoted to commander.

Curita, El. *See* Sergio González

Díaz Argüelles, Raúl (1936–1975) – Member of Revolutionary Directorate from Havana. Joined Directorate guerrilla
column in Escambray mountains 1958. Became Rebel Army
commander 1958. In early 1970s headed Revolutionary Armed
Forces 10th Directorate, which oversaw assistance to Cuba's
internationalist missions. First head of Cuba's military aid to
Angola in 1975. Killed by land mine December 1975. Posthumously promoted to brigadier general. Hero of Republic of
Cuba.

Dreke, Víctor (1937–) – Member of July 26 Movement in Sagua
la Grande, Las Villas; joined Revolutionary Directorate column that integrated into Che Guevara's Rebel Army column
in October 1958. Commanded forces in Escambray mountains in struggle against counterrevolutionary bands 1960–65.
In 1965 was second in command of volunteer column led by
Guevara in Congo. In 1966–68 led Cuban internationalists aiding national liberation forces in Guinea-Bissau. Later headed
Political Directorate of FAR. Retired from active military
duty with rank of colonel. Ambassador to Equatorial Guinea
2003–2008. President of Cuba-Africa Friendship Association
and head of Association of Combatants of Cuban Revolution
in Havana Province.

Espín, Vilma (1930–2007) – Founding member of July 26 Movement in Santiago de Cuba. Collaborator of Frank País, helped
organize November 30, 1956, uprising in Santiago and later
served as July 26 Movement coordinator in Oriente province
following death of País. Joined Rebel Army July 1958, serving
in Second Eastern Front. President of Federation of Cuban

Women from founding in 1960 until her death. Member of Communist Party Central Committee 1965–2007 and Political Bureau 1980–91. Member of Council of State 1976–2007. Heroine of the Republic of Cuba.

Espinosa, Ramón (1939–) – Member of July 26 Movement who joined Revolutionary Directorate guerrilla column in Escambray 1958, finishing war as first lieutenant. Served in Angola 1975–76, seriously wounded by antitank mine. Head of Cuban military mission in Ethiopia 1980–82. Since 2009 vice minister of Revolutionary Armed Forces. Member of Communist Party Central Committee since 1980, Political Bureau since 1991. Holds rank of army corps general. Hero of the Republic of Cuba.

Fontán. *See* Gerardo Abreu

García, Guillermo (1928–) – Peasant from Sierra Maestra who became member of July 26 Movement cell. After landing of *Granma*, helped organize regroupment of rebel forces in Sierra Maestra mountains December 1956. From early 1957, combatant in Column 1 led by Fidel Castro. Promoted to commander in Third Eastern Front led by Juan Almeida, late 1958. Member Communist Party Central Committee since 1965, Political Bureau 1965–86. Minister of transportation 1974–85. Member of Council of State. One of three Sierra combatants to hold title Commander of the Revolution.

Gómez, Máximo (1836–1905) – Born in Dominican Republic, he fought in independence war in Cuba 1868–78. Major general of Liberation Army by end of conflict. When war was relaunched in 1895, returned to Cuba as general heading Cuban independence army.

González, Sergio (El Curita) (1922–1958) – Trade union leader of Havana streetcar workers and bus drivers in late 1940s who joined Orthodox Party. In 1955 became founding member of July 26 Movement. During revolutionary war helped lead urban un-

derground in Havana, managing printshop used by Movement.
Former seminary student, was nicknamed "El Curita" (Little
priest). Murdered March 1958 by Batista dictatorship.

Guevara, Ernesto Che (1928–1967) – Argentine-born leader
of Cuban Revolution. Physician on *Granma* expedition. First
combatant promoted to commander in revolutionary war.
In 1958 led Rebel Army column from Oriente to Escambray
mountains; united revolutionary groups in Las Villas province and led them in campaign culminating in capture of
Santa Clara in late December 1958. After January 1, 1959, triumph, in addition to ongoing military tasks, held responsibilities including head of National Bank and minister of industry;
often represented revolutionary leadership internationally.
From April 1965 led Cuban column fighting alongside anti-
imperialist forces in Congo. In late 1966 led detachment of internationalist volunteers to Bolivia. Wounded and captured
by Bolivian army in CIA-organized operation, October 8, 1967.
Murdered the following day.

Haitian Revolution – Under the impact of the 1789 French
Revolution, a slave insurrection erupted in 1791 in France's
sugar-producing colony of Saint-Domingue. Led by
Toussaint-Louverture and then Jean-Jacques Dessalines, the
rebels abolished slavery and defeated invasions by the French,
Spanish, and British armies. In 1804 they won the establishment of the Republic of Haiti—the second independent nation (after the United States) in the Western Hemisphere and
the world's first black-led republic. The example of the Haitian Revolution terrified plantation owners and inspired enslaved blacks throughout the region, from Louisiana to Cuba
to South America.

Herrera, Osvaldo (1933–1958) – Student leader in the struggle
against Batista. Became Rebel Army captain, serving as adjutant to Commander Camilo Cienfuegos. Sent to Holguín June

1958 to reorganize leadership of July 26 Movement urban underground. Taken prisoner, he committed suicide rather than provide information.

Iraq war (2003) – In March 2003, some 250,000 US and 45,000 British troops invaded Iraq under cover of intense round-the-clock bombing of major cities. Meeting only scattered resistance, the imperialist forces captured Baghdad within three weeks. They overthrew the Baathist regime of Saddam Hussein and began a years-long military occupation of the country. The 2003 war was preceded by the 1990–91 US-led war against Iraq and followed by 12 years of imperialist bombings and economic sanctions against that nation.

ISSCO – International Society for the Study of Chinese Overseas, founded at 1992 conference in San Francisco at initiative of Wang Gungwu of National University of Singapore and Ling-chi Wang, head of Ethnic Studies at University of California in Berkeley. Brings together professors and researchers from around the world who study the Chinese diaspora.

Jordan, Thomas (1819–1895) – General in Confederate Army during US Civil War. In 1869 as supporter of Cuban independence movement, led expedition of 300 men that landed in Cuba. Became general in Liberation Army and chief of staff. Later returned to United States.

July 26 Revolutionary Movement – Founded June 1955 by Fidel Castro and other participants in Moncada attack, fusing with other revolutionary forces, including Revolutionary National Action (ANR) led by Frank País and Revolutionary National Movement (MNR) led by Armando Hart and Faustino Pérez. In May 1958 national leadership was centralized in Sierra Maestra, with Fidel Castro serving as general secretary in addition to Rebel Army commander in chief. Led fusion with Popular Socialist Party and Revolutionary Directorate in 1961 as step toward founding Communist Party of Cuba in 1965.

Kai-shek, Chiang – *See* Chiang Kai-shek

Kuomintang (Nationalist Party) – *See* Chiang Kai-shek

Lazo, Esteban (1944–) – A farmworker from Matanzas, was
founding member of Association of Rebel Youth after 1959 victory. Participated in 1961 literacy campaign. Joined predeces-
sor of Communist Party in 1963. Member of party's Political
Bureau since 1986; head of its department of political education and orientation, 2003–2013. Vice president of Council of
State since 1992. Party first secretary in City of Havana province 1994–2003. President of National Assembly of People's
Power since 2013.

Leyva, Enio (1936–) – Leader of July 26 Movement Youth Brigades, responsible for organizing in high schools. In 1956 became head of action and sabotage in Havana. While training
to be part of *Granma* expedition, was arrested by police in
Mexico. Returned to Cuba 1959. Joined Revolutionary Armed
Forces. Holds rank of brigadier general (retired).

López, Antonio ("Ñico") (1934–1956) – Leader of Orthodox
youth movement. Participated in July 26, 1953, attack on Ba-
yamo garrison. Escaped arrest and went to Guatemala. Met
Ernesto Guevara there in 1954 and helped win him to July 26
Movement. In 1955–56 was member of Movement's National
Directorate and headed its Youth Brigades. Participated in
Granma expedition in December 1956. Captured and mur-
dered by army shortly after landing.

López Cuba, Néstor (1938–1999) – From peasant family in
Holguín. Joined July 26 Movement in 1957 and Rebel Army
in May 1958. Wounded while heading tank unit at Playa
Girón. Served on internationalist missions in Syria 1973,
Angola 1975–76. After 1979 headed Cuba's military mission
to Nicaragua during war against US-backed counterrevolutionary forces. At his death a division general of FAR, member of Central Committee of Communist Party, and chief

executive officer of Association of Combatants of the Cuban Revolution.

Maceo, Antonio (1845–1896) – Military leader in Cuba's 19th century wars of independence from Spain. Known in Cuba as the Bronze Titan, led 1895–96 westward march from Oriente that reached Pinar del Río province. At conclusion of first war in 1878, became symbol of revolutionary intransigence by refusing to put down arms in an action that became known as the Baraguá Protest. Killed in battle.

Machado, Gerardo (1871–1939) – Elected Cuba's president in 1924. Forcibly extended term in office in 1927, unleashing protests across Cuba, which were brutally suppressed. Led US-backed dictatorship 1927–33. August 1933 revolutionary upsurge brought down dictatorship and sent him into exile.

Mambises – Fighters in Cuba's three wars of independence from Spain between 1868 and 1898. Many were escaped or freed slaves and escaped Chinese indentured workers. The term *mambí* is of African origin.

Mandela, Nelson (1918–2013) – Led African National Congress in anti-apartheid struggle in South Africa from 1940s. Arrested 1962, imprisoned until 1990. Released after more than 27 years amid advancing mass struggle, given major boost by 1988 defeat of apartheid army in Angola. Elected president of South Africa 1994 in first post-apartheid election, serving until 1999.

Marcano, Luis (1831–1870) – Born in Dominican Republic, he became general in Cuban independence army. Killed in battle.

March, Aleida (1934–) – Member of July 26 Movement urban underground in Las Villas. In late 1958 went to Escambray mountains. Joined Rebel Army Column 8. Widow of Ernesto Che Guevara.

Márquez, Juan Manuel (1915–1956) – Imprisoned during 1930s for opposing Machado dictatorship. A founding leader in 1947 of Orthodox Party and its left wing. Joined July 26 Movement 1955. Second in command of *Granma* expedition. Captured days after landing and murdered.

Martí, José (1853–1895) – Cuba's national hero. Poet and writer, arrested and exiled for independence activity at age 16. Founded Cuban Revolutionary Party 1892. Led fight to oppose Spanish colonial rule and US designs on Cuba. Organized 1895 independence war. Killed in battle.

Martínez Gil, Pascual (1943–2014) – Member of July 26 Movement during struggle against Batista. Headed Ministry of Interior Special Troops in Angola 1975. Member of Communist Party Central Committee 1980–89, deputy minister of interior 1980– 89. Held rank of division general. Arrested 1989 on charges of abuse of authority and improper use of government funds and resources; sentenced to 12-year prison term.

Martínez Hierrezuelo, Miguel Mariano – Combatant in July 26 Movement's clandestine struggle in Santiago de Cuba. Participated in November 30, 1956, uprising in support of *Granma* landing. Served in Rebel Army Column 1 under Fidel Castro; later in Third Front commanded by Juan Almeida.

Masetti, Jorge Ricardo (1929–1964) – Argentine journalist who went to Sierra Maestra January 1958 and was won to Rebel cause. Founded Cuba's Prensa Latina news service. Lost and presumed dead while leading guerrilla front in northern Argentina; remains never found.

Mella, Julio Antonio (1903–1929) – Founding president of Federation of University Students (FEU) 1923. A founding leader of Communist Party of Cuba 1925. Arrested by Machado's police 1926, escaped to Mexico, continuing to organize against dictatorship. Assassinated in Mexico City by Machado's agents, January 1929.

Moncada attack – On July 26, 1953, some 160 revolutionaries under command of Fidel Castro launched insurrectionary attack on Moncada army garrison in Santiago de Cuba and simultaneous attack on garrison in Bayamo, opening revolutionary armed struggle against Batista dictatorship. Five died in combat at Moncada. After action failed to take garrison, Batista forces massacred 56 captured revolutionaries. Fidel Castro, Raúl Castro, Juan Almeida, and 25 others captured, tried, and sentenced to up to 15 years in prison. They were amnestied May 15, 1955, after a broad national campaign demanding their release.

Moracén, Rafael (1939–) – Joined Rebel Army 1958. Served on internationalist missions in Congo-Brazzaville 1965–67, Syria 1973, Angola 1975–82. Holds rank of brigadier general (retired). Hero of the Republic of Cuba. Served as head of international relations for Association of Combatants of Cuban Revolution.

País, Frank (1934–1957) – Vice president of Federation of University Students in Oriente. Central leader of Revolutionary National Action (ANR) and later of Revolutionary National Movement (MNR). In September 1955 MNR joined July 26 Movement and País became its central leader in Oriente province, national action coordinator, and head of urban militias. Murdered by dictatorship's forces July 30, 1957.

Pardo Guerra, Ramón (1939–) – Joined Rebel Army 1957; served in Column 8 under Che Guevara 1958. Member of Communist Party Central Committee 1965–86 and since 1997. Served internationalist mission in Angola 1980. Head of national general staff of civil defense since 2002. Holds rank of division general.

Paz, Ramón (1924–1958) – Member of July 26 Movement and Rebel Army commander in Column 1. Killed in battle of Providencia, July 28, 1958.

Pérez, Crescencio (1895–1986) – A member of July 26 Movement cell in Sierra Maestra prior to *Granma* landing. One of first peasants to join Rebel Army, finishing war as commander of Column 7. Following triumph of revolution, carried various responsibilities in Revolutionary Armed Forces.

Pérez Jiménez, Marcos (1914–2001) – Military dictator of Venezuela from 1952 until toppled in popular rebellion in January 1958.

Pino Machado, Quintín (1931–1986) – Member of July 26 Movement in Las Villas during revolutionary war. After 1959 Cuba's ambassador to Nicaragua 1959–60, representative to Organization of American States, and vice minister of culture.

Plácido – Literary pseudonym of poet Gabriel de la Concepción Valdés (1809–1844). A free black, he was arrested by Spanish colonial authorities, framed as ringleader of "Ladder Conspiracy" to start slave uprising, and executed by firing squad.

Playa Girón – On April 17, 1961, 1,500 Cuban mercenaries organized, financed, and deployed by Washington invaded Cuba at Bay of Pigs on southern coast. In less than seventy-two hours they were defeated by Cuba's revolutionary militias, armed forces, and police. Remaining invaders were captured at Playa Girón (Girón Beach), the name Cubans use for the invasion and battle.

Popular Socialist Party (PSP) – Name taken in 1944 by Communist Party of Cuba. PSP opposed Batista dictatorship but rejected political course of Moncada assault and of July 26 Movement and Rebel Army in launching revolutionary war in 1956–57. PSP cadres collaborated with July 26 Movement in final months of struggle to topple dictatorship. After 1959 victory, July 26 Movement initiated fusion with PSP and Revolutionary Directorate in 1961, leading to founding of Communist Party of Cuba in 1965.

Portuguese revolution – In April 1974 military coup in Portugal overthrew decaying fascist dictatorship of Marcelo Caetano, unleashing mass popular upsurge known as "Carnation Revolution." Advancing independence struggles in

African colonies, especially in Guinea-Bissau, and growing opposition within Portugal to attempts to crush anticolonial movements were central to regime's fall.

Quesada, Gonzalo de (1868–1915) – Secretary of Cuban Revolutionary Party from founding in 1892. Representative in Washington of Cuban Republic in Arms during 1895–98 independence war. Later helped publish collected works of José Martí.

Ramos Latour, René (Daniel) (1932–1958) – Joined July 26 Movement 1955. Member of Rebel Army's first reinforcement detachment March 1957. Returned to Santiago de Cuba to help lead urban underground struggle, became July 26 Movement national action coordinator after Frank País's death July 1957. Returned to Sierra Maestra May 1958, becomes commander of a column. Killed in battle July 30, 1958, at end of Batista army's offensive in Sierra Maestra.

Reeve, Henry ("El Inglesito") (1850–1876) – Union Army drummerboy during US Civil War. Went to Cuba and joined independence forces in 1869, inspired by Cubans' fight against slavery. Became a colonel and was named commander of Cienfuegos detachment of independence army. Killed in battle.

Republic in Arms – Created by Cuban independence forces in April 1869 at Guáimaro Assembly, to lead war against Spanish colonialism. First president was Carlos Manuel de Céspedes. Decreed abolition of slavery and indentured servitude.

Revolution of 1933 – Revolutionary upsurge and general strike that toppled Machado dictatorship in August 1933. Replaced by proimperialist regime led by Carlos Manuel de Céspedes, son of the initiator of Cuba's 1868 independence war; toppled same year in a coup led by noncommissioned officers, students, and civilians known as "Sergeants' Revolt." "Hundred Days" coalition government formed; included antiimperialist leaders such as Antonio Guiteras; decreed eight-hour day; annulled US "right to intervene" in Cuba (Platt Amendment). With support of US embassy, army chief of staff Fulgencio Batista led second coup January 14, 1934, which ended revolutionary government.

Revolutionary Directorate – Founded 1955 by José Antonio Echeverría and other leaders of Federation of University Students. In 1956 in Mexico, signed agreement with July 26 Movement to cooperate in actions against dictatorship. Organized March 13, 1957, attack on Presidential Palace; some 40 members and leaders, including Echeverría, were killed that day and in cop massacre several weeks later. In October 1958 its guerrilla column in Escambray mountains joined front commanded by Che Guevara. Fused with July 26 Movement and Popular Socialist Party in 1961.

Rius Rivera, Juan (1848–1924) – Native of Puerto Rico who joined Cuba's independence war in 1870. With resumption of war in 1895, sought to organize armed expedition to fight for Puerto Rico's independence. When plan failed, led armed expedition to Cuba and joined independence army. Became a major general.

Rodríguez, René (1931–1990) – Member of revolutionary movement led by Fidel Castro in 1952–53. *Granma* expeditionary in 1956. Served in Column 8 under Che Guevara. Promoted to commander in 1959. Headed Cuban Institute for Friendship with the Peoples (ICAP) 1977–90. Member of Communist Party Central Committee from 1980 until his death.

Rodríguez Nodals, Adolfo (1945–2017) – Director of Institute of Basic Research on Tropical Agriculture (INIFAT). Head of National Urban Agriculture Group in Cuba.

Roloff, Carlos (1842–1907) – Born in Poland, he went to US to fight in Union Army during Civil War. Went to Cuba in 1865, became a fighter in Cuban independence army in 1868. In 1890s was chairman of Cuban Revolutionary Party in Tampa,

Florida. When war was relaunched in 1895, returned to Cuba and became major general in Liberation Army.

Rosales del Toro, Ulises (1942–) – Joined Rebel Army 1957, serving under Juan Almeida. Served in internationalist missions in Algeria and Venezuela 1963–68, and Angola 1976. A member of Communist Party Central Committee since 1975 and of party's Political Bureau 1986–2011. Minister of sugar industry 1997–2009, minister of agriculture 2008–10. Vice president of Council of Ministers. Holds rank of division general.

Salcines, Miguel (1950–) – Irrigation specialist for Ministry of Agriculture. As head of a UBPC, developed urban agriculture projects in Cuba, and collaborated in one in Venezuela.

Savimbi, Jonas (1934–2002) – Led faction of Angola's independence movement from 1960. Founding leader of UNITA 1966. From 1975, allied with Pretoria and Washington to overturn MPLA-led government. After 1988 defeat of South African intervention, continued war against Luanda. Killed in battle, leading to cease-fire in 27-year war. *See also* UNITA.

Schueg, Víctor (1936–1998) – Joined Rebel Army 1958, serving under Raúl Castro. Internationalist missions in Congo 1965, in Angola 1975–76 chief of general staff of military mission. Head of Central Army 1987–88. Held rank of brigadier general in FAR. Alternate member of Communist Party Central Committee 1980–86, full member 1986–91.

Second National Front of the Escambray – Armed group in Las Villas led by Eloy Gutiérrez Menoyo. Formed November 1957 on initiative of Revolutionary Directorate but expelled by Directorate in mid-1958 for terrorizing peasants in Escambray. Refused to collaborate with Rebel Army forces led by Che Guevara and other revolutionary units. After 1959 most of its leaders joined counterrevolution.

Sékou Touré, Ahmed (1922–1984) – Leader of independence struggle from France in what is today Guinea-Conakry. Became president of country at independence in 1958, serving until his death.

Slavery in Cuba – First brought to Cuba in 1517 by Spanish crown, slaves were principal source of labor in the sugar industry, constituting over a third of Cuban population by 1840s. Fear of slave revolts and international treaties banning slave trade from 1817, as sugar production in Cuba expanded, fostered "coolie" trade bringing in some 125,000 Chinese indentured laborers between 1847 and 1874. In 1869, during first war for liberation from Spain, the Republic in Arms decreed abolition of slavery and all forms of bonded servitude, incorporating all who wanted to fight into independence army. Spain decreed gradual elimination of slavery in 1870 and in 1880 declared all remaining slaves to be bonded laborers under *patronato* system. On October 7, 1886, the remaining 25,000 *patrocinados* were emancipated.

Special Period – Term in Cuba for severe economic conditions in 1990s and revolutionary government's course to address them. With disintegration of USSR and fall of allied Eastern and Central European regimes, Cuba lost 85 percent of its foreign trade, leading to estimated 35 percent decline in gross domestic product. Shortages of food and other essentials were amplified by world capitalist crisis and stepped-up US economic warfare. By 1996 efforts by Cuban working people and government began to revive farm and industrial output, though far below pre-1990 levels.

Sumner Welles, Benjamin (1892–1962) – US assistant secretary of state sent by President Franklin Roosevelt as ambassador to Cuba in 1933 to organize transfer of power from dictator Gerardo Machado and put an end to revolutionary upsurge. *See* Revolution of 1933.

SWAPO (South-West Africa People's Organisation) – Formed 1960, led fight for Namibia's independence from South Africa;

founding leader was Sam Nujoma. Fought alongside Cuban-Angolan forces on Angola's southern front. Governing party in Namibia since independence in 1990.

Territorial Troop Militia – Nationwide volunteer militia organized 1980 in wake of Grenadian and Nicaraguan revolutionary victories to help defend Cuba from heightened threats of imperialist attack. Composed of 1.5 million workers, farmers, students, and housewives, who train on their own time and help finance their military expenses.

Tito, Josip Broz (1892–1980) – Head of Yugoslav Communist Party from 1939. Led partisan movement against Nazi occupation during World War II. Prime minister and later president of Yugoslavia 1945–80.

Tolón, José (Lai Wa) – Chinese-born officer in Cuban independence army, fighting in Cuba's three wars against Spanish colonial rule. Reached rank of captain.

Torres, Félix (1917–2008) – Commanded PSP guerrilla column in Yaguajay, northern Las Villas; collaborated with Camilo Cienfuegos's Rebel Army column in late 1958.

Trejo, Rafael (1910–1930) – Vice president of Law Students Association at University of Havana. Killed by police September 30, 1930, during demonstration against Machado dictatorship.

UNITA (National Union for the Total Independence of Angola) – Founded 1966 to fight Portuguese rule, led by Jonas Savimbi. In 1975 allied with apartheid South Africa and Washington to overthrow MPLA-led government of newly independent Angola. For 27 years waged war against Luanda. Signed cease-fire in 2002, after Savimbi was killed in battle.

Urgency Courts – Formed in June 1934 under first Batista regime, courts were set up to try and jail Batista's opponents. Abolished after triumph of revolution.

Valdés, Ramiro (1932–) – A truck driver and carpenter, he participated in 1953 Moncada attack. Sentenced to ten years in prison. Released May 1955 following amnesty campaign. *Granma* expeditionary. Became second in command of Rebel Army Column 4 in Sierra Maestra, later becoming its commander, and second in command of Column 8 under Guevara in Las Villas. Minister of interior 1961–68, 1979–85. Member of Communist Party Central Committee since 1965, Political Bureau 1965–86. One of three Sierra combatants to hold title Commander of the Revolution. Vice president of Council of Ministers.

Van Heerden, Neil (1939–) – Head of apartheid South Africa's Ministry of Foreign Affairs in 1980s. Involved in negotiations with Cuba and Angola over end of war. From 1996 to 2005 served as executive director of a foundation representing 60 of country's largest corporations.

Villegas, Harry (Pombo) (1940–) – Joined Rebel Army 1957, becoming member of Che Guevara's escort in Columns 4 and 8. Served with Guevara in Congo 1965 and later Bolivia 1966–67, where he was a member of the general staff of the guerrilla movement. After Guevara was captured and killed in October 1967, led group of six surviving combatants who eluded encirclement by Bolivian army. Returned to Cuba March 1968. Served three tours of duty in Angola in 1970s and 1980s. Brigadier general (retired) in Revolutionary Armed Forces, member of Central Committee of Communist Party 1997–2011. Executive vice president of Association of Combatants of the Cuban Revolution 1999–2012. Hero of the Republic of Cuba.

Wang Gungwu (1930–) – Historian and founding president of International Society for the Study of Chinese Overseas 1992. Has written extensively on the Chinese diaspora. Professor at National University of Singapore and chair of its East Asian Institute.

Wang, Ling-chi (1938–) – A founding leader of International Society for the Study of Chinese Overseas 1992. In late 1960s helped lead struggle by students that won establishment of Asian American studies at University of California (Berkeley) and other campuses. For many years the chair of UC Berkeley's Ethnic Studies Department.

Wong, José (Huan Taobai, c. 1898–1930) – Revolutionary from Canton, China, who came to Cuba in early 1920s. In 1927 was a founding leader of Revolutionary Alliance for the Protection of Chinese Workers and Peasants in Cuba. Joined Communist Party of Cuba and founded Chinese-language newspaper *Gunnun Hushen* (Worker-Peasant Call), serving as its editor. In May 1930 was arrested and imprisoned in Havana's Príncipe prison together with other Communist Party leaders. Three months later he was strangled to death in jail cell by agents of Machado dictatorship.

Youth Army of Labor (EJT) – Part of Cuba's Revolutionary Armed Forces, composed of detachments of youth who carry out agricultural, construction, and other work at same time as they train militarily. Members receive pay corresponding to type of work they do.

Yugoslavia, US-led war against – Culminating a decade of military assaults on Yugoslavia, in 1999 Washington and NATO allies waged 80-day bombing of Serbia and Kosova that killed and maimed thousands and devastated factories and infrastructure. Aiming to overturn the conquests of the 1945 Yugoslav revolution, the imperialists took advantage of wars between rival bureaucratic ruling layers in Serbia, Croatia, and other regions. The occupation and dismemberment of that country reinforced Washington's dominance in Europe and led to further eastward expansion of NATO, bringing US military might closer to the borders of Russia.

Index

213

UNITA (National Union for the
Total Independence of Angola),
99–100, 110–11, 121, 207, 209
United Fruit Company, 143
United States, 75
anti–Vietnam War movement
in, 130
Chinese in, 10, 23, 78–79, 91
cultural influence of, 184
immigration to, 179
natural disasters in, 25–26, 139
University of Havana, 60–61, 96
Urban agriculture
in Cuba, 143, 148–58
organopónicos, origin of term,
149
in Venezuela, 25, 40, 176–77, 179
Urgency Courts, 48, 209
US imperialism, 11, 89–90, 122–23
and Angola, 99, 110
attacks and threats against Cuba,
24, 125, 127, 130, 134–35, 178,
187
military power of, 24, 108, 116
and Venezuela, 178
Yugoslavia and Iraq wars, 129–30

Valdés, Ramiro, 108, 209–10
Valladares, Pepe, 92
Van Heerden, Neil, 113–14, 210
Vegetables
Cuba as importer of, 146, 148
and Cuban diet, 156–57
See also Urban agriculture
Venezuela, 151
capitalist opposition in, 170–71,
177–78
education programs, 173–74
health care programs, 172, 174–75
oil wealth of, 169–72
social conditions in, 170–71
support for Chávez in, 179–82
Vargas disaster, 172
working people of, 171, 181
in world politics, 172

Venezuela, Cuban assistance, 103,
169, 180–81
doctors, 169, 172–75, 177–81
literacy effort, 173–74
sports instructors, 169, 175
and urban agriculture, 24, 40,
176–77, 179–80
Vietnam, 130, 135
Villegas, Harry (Pombo), 21, 210

Wages, 150–51, 153, 165
Wang Gungwu, 95–96, 199, 210
Wang, Ling-chi, 95–96, 199, 210–11
Wang Lusha, 11–12, 15–20
Wanton, Lidia, 56
War of the entire people, 128
Waters, Mary-Alice, 16
Welles, Sumner, 90
Women, 92, 96, 153
in Chinese immigration, 85
Wong, José, 18, 92, 211
Wong, Rafael, 54
Workers
agricultural, 150–53
in anti-Batista struggle, 49, 61–62
Cuban revolution as example
for, 24
and socialist revolution, 154,
170–71
stevedores, 164–66
Wyatt Earp (film), 79

Yeltsin, Boris, 133
Yemen, 103
Youth, 153, 173
alienation among, 185
in anti-Batista struggle, 47, 56,
60–62
political education of, 123–24, 181,
183, 186–88
Youth Army of Labor (EJT), 158,
211
Yugoslavia, 129–30

Zaire, 99, 108, 111, 121

Workers and the US rulers'

Three books for today's spreading and deepening debate among working people looking for a way forward in face of capitalism's global economic and social calamity and wars.

The Clintons' Anti-Working-Class Record

Why Washington Fears Working People

Jack Barnes

Hillary Clinton calls workers who refused to vote for her "deplorables." Donald Trump uses demagogy to try to turn working people against each other. Barnes documents US capitalism's drive for profits over the last quarter century and the consequences for working people, who want to "drain the swamp" of capitalist politics as usual.

$10. Also in Spanish, French, and Farsi.

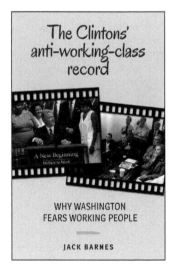

deepening political crisis

Are They Rich Because They're Smart?

Class, Privilege, and Learning under Capitalism

Jack Barnes

Takes apart self-serving rationalizations by layers of well-paid professionals that their intelligence and schooling equip them to "regulate" the lives of working people, who don't know our own best interests.

$10. Also in Spanish, French, and Farsi.

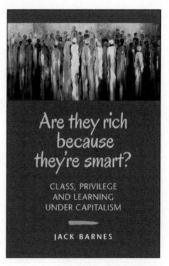

Is Socialist Revolution in the US Possible?

A Necessary Debate among Working People

Mary-Alice Waters

An unhesitating "Yes"—that's the answer by Waters. Possible—but not inevitable. That depends on us.

$10. Also in Spanish, French, and Farsi.

Marx and Engels on China and the Opium Wars

"Before many years pass away, we shall have to witness the death-struggle of the oldest empire in the world, and the opening day of a new era for all Asia."

Articles by Marx and Engels from the 1850s on European capitalism's plunder of China, the second Opium War waged by the colonial powers, and the place of the wealth and labor power wrested from China in the worldwide accumulation of capital.

In *Collected Works of Karl Marx and Frederick Engels*, volumes 15 and 16. $35 each.

Cuba's Socialist Revolution and the World

Cuba and Angola:
The War for Freedom

HARRY VILLEGAS ("POMBO")

The story of Cuba's unparalleled contribution to the fight to free Africa from the scourge of apartheid. And how, in the doing, Cuba's socialist revolution was strengthened.

$10. Also in Spanish.

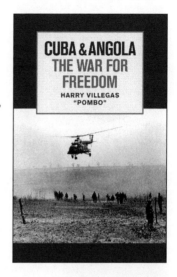

Companion volume

Cuba and Angola

Fighting for Africa's Freedom and Our Own

FIDEL CASTRO, RAÚL CASTRO, NELSON MANDELA, AND OTHERS

$12. Also in Spanish.

How Far We Slaves Have Come!
South Africa and Cuba in Today's World

NELSON MANDELA, FIDEL CASTRO

Speaking together in Cuba in 1991, Mandela and Castro discuss the place in the history of Africa of the victory by Cuban, Angolan, and Namibian combatants over the US-backed South African army that had invaded Angola.

$10. Also in Spanish and Farsi.

Women in Cuba:
The Making of a Revolution
within the Revolution

VILMA ESPÍN, ASELA DE LOS SANTOS, YOLANDA FERRER

The integration of women into the ranks and leadership of the Cuban Revolution was inseparably intertwined with the proletarian course of the revolution from the start. This is the story of that revolution and how it transformed the women and men who made it.

$20. Also in Spanish and Greek.

Revolutionary leaders

Cuba and the Coming American Revolution
Jack Barnes

This is a book about the struggles of working people in the imperialist heartland, the youth attracted to them, and the example set by the Cuban people that revolution is not only necessary—it can be made. It is about the class struggle in the US, where the revolutionary capacities of workers and farmers are today as utterly discounted by the ruling powers as were those of the Cuban toilers. And just as wrongly.
$10. Also in Spanish, French, and Farsi.

Malcolm X Talks to Young People

"The young generation of whites, Blacks, browns, whatever else there is—you're living at a time of revolution," Malcolm said in December 1964. "And I for one will join in with anyone, I don't care what color you are, as long as you want to change this miserable condition that exists on this earth." Four talks and an interview given to young people in the last months of Malcolm's life.
$15. Also in Spanish, French, Farsi, and Greek.

Aldabonazo
Inside the Cuban Revolutionary Underground
1952–58
Armando Hart

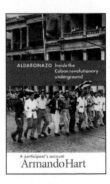

In this account by a historic leader of the Cuban Revolution, we meet men and women who led the urban underground in the fight against the US-backed tyranny in the 1950s. Together with the Rebel Army, they not only overthrew the dictatorship. Their revolutionary actions and example worldwide changed the history of the 20th century—and the century to come.
$25. Also in Spanish.

... in their own words

Teamster Politics
Farrell Dobbs

Tells how Teamster Local 544 organized
the unemployed and truck owner-
operators into fighting union auxiliaries.
Deployed a Union Defense Guard
to respond to the fascist Silver Shirts.
Combated FBI frame-ups. Campaigned
for workers to break politically from the
bosses and organize a labor party based
on the unions. And mobilized labor
opposition to US imperialism's entry into
World War II. $19. Also in Spanish.

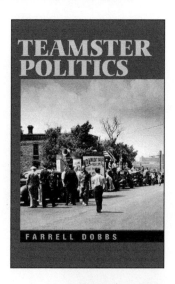

Episodes of the Cuban Revolutionary War, 1956–58
Ernesto Che Guevara

A firsthand account of political events and military
campaigns that culminated in the January 1959 popular
insurrection that overthrew the US-backed dictatorship
in Cuba. With clarity and humor, Guevara describes his
own political education. He explains how the struggle
transformed the men and women of the Rebel Army
and July 26 Movement, opening the door to the first
socialist revolution in the Americas. $30

Thomas Sankara Speaks
The Burkina Faso Revolution, 1983–87

In 1983 the peasants and workers of Burkina Faso
established a popular revolutionary government
and began to combat the colonial legacy of hunger,
illiteracy, and economic backwardness. Thomas
Sankara, who led that struggle, explains the example
set for Africa and the world. $24. Also in French.

Also from Pathfinder

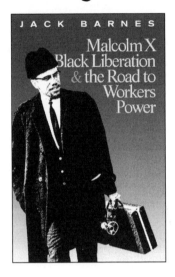

Malcolm X, Black Liberation, and the Road to Workers Power
Jack Barnes

Drawing lessons from a century and a half of struggle, this book helps us understand why it is the revolutionary conquest of power by the working class that will make possible the final battle against class exploitation and racist oppression and open the way to a world based on human solidarity. A socialist world.
$20. Also in Spanish, French, Farsi, Arabic, and Greek.

The Communist Manifesto
Karl Marx and Frederick Engels

Why communism is not a set of preconceived principles but the line of march of the working class toward power, "springing from an existing class struggle, a historical movement going on under our very eyes." The founding document of the modern revolutionary workers movement.
$5. Also in Spanish, French, Farsi, and Arabic.

Lenin's Final Fight
Speeches and Writings, 1922–23
V.I. Lenin

In 1922 and 1923, V.I. Lenin, central leader of the world's first socialist revolution, waged what was to be his last political battle—one that was lost following his death. At stake was whether that revolution, and the international movement it led, would remain on the proletarian course that had brought workers and peasants to power in October 1917.
$20. Also in Spanish and Greek.

U.S. Imperialism
Has Lost the Cold War
Jack Barnes

The collapse a quarter century ago of
regimes across Eastern Europe and the
USSR claiming to be communist did
not mean workers and farmers there
had been crushed. In today's sharpening
inter-capitalist conflicts and wars,
these toilers become an intractable
obstacle to capitalism's advance. In *New
International* no. 11.
$16. Also in Spanish, French, Farsi, and
Greek.

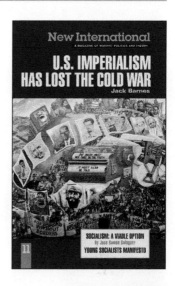

From the Escambray to the Congo
In the Whirlwind of the Cuban Revolution
Víctor Dreke

A leading participant in Cuba's revolutionary
movement for more than half a century describes
his experiences as second-in-command in the 1965
internationalist mission in Congo led by Che
Guevara. He describes the creative joy of working
people in Cuba, at home and abroad, as they've
defended their revolutionary course.
$18. Also in Spanish.

Puerto Rico:
Independence Is a Necessity
Rafael Cancel Miranda

One of the five Puerto Rican Nationalists imprisoned
by Washington for more than 25 years and released in
1979 speaks out on the brutal reality of US colonial
domination, the campaign to free Puerto Rican
political prisoners, the example of Cuba's socialist
revolution, and the ongoing struggle for independence.
$6. Also in Spanish and Farsi.

EXPAND YOUR REVOLUTIONARY LIBRARY

Our Politics
Start with the World

JACK BARNES

The huge economic and cultural inequalities between imperialist and semicolonial countries, and among classes within them, are reproduced and accentuated by the workings of capitalism. For vanguard workers to build parties able to lead a successful revolutionary struggle for power in our own countries, our activity must be guided by a strategy to close this gap. $14. Also in Spanish, French, Farsi, and Greek.

Leon Trotsky on China

Articles and letters on the Chinese revolution of 1925–27. Trotsky records the fight to reverse the disastrous course of the Stalin-led Communist International of subordinating working people there to the leadership of the capitalist-landlord Chinese Nationalist Party (Kuomintang). $35

Playa Girón/Bay of Pigs
Washington's First Military Defeat in the Americas

FIDEL CASTRO, JOSÉ RAMÓN FERNÁNDEZ

In fewer than 72 hours of combat in April 1961, Cuba's revolutionary armed forces defeated a US-organized invasion by 1,500 mercenaries. In the process, the Cuban people set an example for workers, farmers, and youth the world over that with political consciousness, class solidarity, courage, and revolutionary leadership, we can stand up to enormous might and seemingly insurmountable odds—and win. $22. Also in Spanish.

"It's the Poor Who Face the Savagery of the US 'Justice' System"

The Cuban Five Talk about Their Lives within the US Working Class

From police to courts to prisons to parole: how the US "justice" system works as "an enormous machine for grinding people up." Five Cuban revolutionaries—framed up by the US government and incarcerated for 16 years—draw on their own experience to explain the human devastation wrought by capitalist "justice." And what makes socialist Cuba different. $15. Also in Spanish, Farsi, and Greek.

Socialism on Trial
Testimony at Minneapolis Sedition Trial
JAMES P. CANNON

The revolutionary program of the working class, as presented in response to frame-up charges of "seditious conspiracy" in 1941, on the eve of US entry into World War II. The defendants were leaders of the Minneapolis labor movement and the Socialist Workers Party. Includes Cannon's answer to ultraleft critics. $16. Also in Spanish, French, and Farsi.

Cosmetics, Fashions, and the Exploitation of Women
JOSEPH HANSEN, EVELYN REED, MARY-ALICE WATERS

How big business plays on women's second-class status and economic insecurities to market cosmetics and rake in profits. And how the entry of millions of women into the workforce has irreversibly changed relations between women and men—for the better. $15. Also in Spanish and Farsi.

WWW.PATHFINDERPRESS.COM

PATHFINDER AROUND THE WORLD

Visit our website for a complete list of titles and to place orders

www.pathfinderpress.com

PATHFINDER DISTRIBUTORS

UNITED STATES
(and Caribbean, Latin America, and East Asia)

Pathfinder Books, 306 W. 37th St., 13th Floor
New York, NY 10018

CANADA

Pathfinder Books, 7107 St. Denis, Suite 204
Montreal, QC H2S 2S5

UNITED KINGDOM
(and Europe, Africa, Middle East, and South Asia)

Pathfinder Books, 2nd Floor, 83 Kingsland High St.
Dalston, London, E8 2PB

AUSTRALIA
(and Southeast Asia and the Pacific)

Pathfinder, Level 1, 3/281–287 Beamish St., Campsie, NSW 2194
Postal address: P.O. Box 164, Campsie, NSW 2194

NEW ZEALAND

Pathfinder, 188a Onehunga Mall Rd., Onehunga, Auckland 1061
Postal address: P.O. Box 13857, Auckland 1643

PATHFINDER READERS CLUB • CLUB DE LECTORES

NAME
NOMBRE

EXPIRATION DATE • FECHA QUE VENCE: ___/___/___

Valid at Pathfinder book centers and online
Válido en centros de libros Pathfinder y en línea
www.pathfinderpress.com